FUN

PICKLING

BY

DANIEL ISACCS

TABLE OF CONTENTS

CHAPTER ONE

PICKLING

Pickling is the process of preserving or expanding the lifespan of food by either anaerobic fermentation in brine or immersion in vinegar. The resulting food is called a pickle, or, to prevent ambiguity, prefaced with the adjective pickled. The pickling procedure will typically affect the food's texture and flavor. In East Asia, vinaigrette (vegetable oil and vinegar) is also used as a pickling medium. Foods that are pickled include meats, fruits, eggs, and vegetables.

Another distinguishing characteristic is a pH of 4.6 or lower, which is sufficient to kill most bacteria. Pickling can preserve perishable foods for months. Antimicrobial herbs and spices, such as mustard seed, garlic, cinnamon or cloves, are often added. If the food contains sufficient moisture, a pickling brine may be produced simply by adding dry salt. For example, German sauerkraut and Korean kimchi are produced by salting the vegetables to draw out excess water. Natural fermentation at room temperature, by lactic acid bacteria, produces the required acidity. Other pickles are made by placing vegetables in vinegar. Unlike the canning process, pickling (which includes fermentation) does not require that the food be completely sterile before it is sealed. The acidity or salinity of the solution, the temperature of fermentation, and the exclusion of oxygen determine which microorganisms dominate, and determine the flavor of the end product.

When both salt concentration and temperature are low, Leuconostoc mesenteroides dominates, producing a mix of acids, alcohol, and aroma compounds. At higher temperatures Lactobacillus plantarum dominates, which produces primarily lactic acid. Many pickles start with Leuconostoc, and change to Lactobacillus with higher acidity.

History of pickling

Pickling began 4000 years ago using cucumbers native to India.[citation needed] This was used as a way to preserve food for out-of-season use and for long journeys, especially by sea. Salt pork and salt beef were common staples for sailors before the days of steam engines. Although the process was invented to preserve foods, pickles are also made and eaten because people enjoy the resulting flavors. Pickling may also improve the nutritional value of food by introducing B vitamins produced by bacteria.

The term pickle is derived from the Dutch word pekel, meaning brine. In the U.S. and Canada, and sometimes Australia and New Zealand, the word pickle alone almost always refers to a pickled cucumber, except when it is used figuratively. It may also refer to other types of pickles such as "pickled onion", "pickled cauliflower", etc. In the UK, pickle, as in a "cheese and pickle sandwich", may also refer to Ploughman's pickle, a kind of chutney.

10 Benefits of Naturally Pickled and Fermented Foods

Natural pickling and fermentation are the most unique, traditional forms of food preservation that enhances the q uality of the foods. Fermentation is an external, predigestion process that converts complex nutrients to simpler ones. Common fermented foods and beverages include sourdough, vinegar, and wine. Pickling is a type of controlled fermentation using salt. Examples of pickled products are miso, sauerkraut, and olives.

Modern preservation techniq ues stop the changes in foods. In essence, these foods become sterile. Natural pickling and fermentation facilitates continuous, ongoing transformation and enhancement of certain aspects of foods. For example, pressed apples (apple cider), if unpasteurized, over time ferments into hard apple cider, an alcoholic beverage. If left to further ferment, hard apple cider turns into apple cider vinegar. Each product is unique, and in some ways, mimics the aging process in human beings. Although the fresh, bright aspects may decline as we lose youth, our deeper, essential qualities become enhanced as we age.

Benefits of Naturally Pickled and Fermented Foods

1) For healthy digestion, we need both prebiotics and probiotics. Prebiotics are the fibers in whole grains, beans, vegetables, and fruits.

2) Pickled and fermented foods, commonly now referred to as sources of probiotics, when combined with prebiotics, help create the healthiest environment for gut microbes to flourish.

3) We have a second nervous system called the enteric nervous system in our gut. It is composed of the same types of cells that make up our central nervous system. Pickled and fermented foods bolster and

support the connection between the cells that are shared between these two nervous systems.

4) We also have two digestive systems. Mental, emotional, and digestive health are interrelated and affected by the foods we eat. Our digestive system processes liq uids whereas the brain and nervous system process thoughts, ideas, and vibrations.

5) Naturally pickled and fermented foods support the development of gut microbes which prevents unhealthy microbes from developing and flourishing.

6) Pickled and fermented foods help develop a natural, efficient immune response, and also suppress inflammatory response often associated with allergies, cardiovascular disease, and cancer.

7) Pickled and fermented foods best express the q ualities of a particular climate. Wine, beer, and miso are common examples of how microclimates affect the quality of a fermented product. If we want to assimilate to another environment, eating or drinking native, naturally pickled and fermented foods help us adapt more easily to that climate.

8) The basis of a healthy plant-based diet are grains, beans, vegetables and fruits. The most important

probiotics for this way of eating are miso (grain and bean), sauerkraut (vegetable), and umeboshi plum (fruit).

9) Pickled and fermented foods aid the digestive process and our ability to absorb and utilize nutrients.

10) It is the interaction of foods that provides the greatest benefit. Pickled and fermented foods should be eaten in combination with other foods during a meal. Having miso soup, sauerkraut or a glass of wine during a meal provides the fullest benefit.

CHAPTER TWO

PICKLING : A BEGINNER'S GUIDE

Pickling any vegetable that's losing its crunch is a surprisingly easy thing to do. With a little vinegar, salt, sugar, and select spices, you can transform aging veggies into a savory stand-alone snack or zesty ingredient to revive a tired recipe. This is also one of the best ways to stretch your produce dollars and preserve summer flavors for the bland, winter months.

What you'll need

Dig out your two biggest cooking pots — one for preparing the pickled vegetables and another for the canning process. You'll want to use the larger pot for boiling and sealing the canning jars. One inch of water should keep the jars covered at all times. Invest in a new case of Ball or Kerr brand canning jars, selecting a size that best fits with your pot. Keep a set of tongs handy to remove hot jars from boiling water.

Choose which vegetables you want to pickle. Typically, veggies with a tougher skin like cucumbers and peppers do best in the pickling process, but root vegetables like carrots and radishes also work well. A good rule of thumb is the sturdier the vegetable, the better.

Stock up on vinegar. Most recipes call for cider vinegar or distilled vinegar. Pull salt, sugar, and dry spices from your pantry and make sure you have enough of each veggie. If you want to boost the flavor, consider buying fresh herbs rather than using dried ones.

Pickling dos and don'ts

• Don't be lured by "European-style" canning jar marketing — these options will only make the process more difficult and expensive.

• Don't buy new cookware if your jars are too big for your largest pot; buy new jars instead. Jars are far less expensive and come in 8-ounce and 16-ounce sizes. You can always find creative ways to use the extra set of jars.

• Do invest in a canning kit that includes wide-grip tongs to make the process go more smoothly. Ball sells a Canning Utensil Set ($10) with jar tongs, a wide funnel to make the jar-filling process easy, and a magnet-tipped wand that helps remove lids from hot water.

• Don't take shortcuts. The jar and lid sterilization process, boiling water timing, and amount of vinegar used are all critical components to crafting perfect pickles.

• Do consider both sweet and salty when making recipes. If you add more vinegar to the pickling liq uid mixture, increase the sugar proportionally to keep the flavor balanced.

Remember that you can always add more vinegar or sugar, but you can't remove any.

• Don't obsess when measuring fresh veggies. You can vary from the recipe's specified amount by a full cup without affecting the outcome. Just try to cut all vegetables to the same relative size and cover them evenly with the pickling liq uid.

• Do get creative! Pickling provides great opportunity to play with a variety of herb, spice, and flavor combos. Blend together a few favorites to create your own pickling recipe others will envy. Just keep in mind that herbs like celery seed, turmeric, and garlic pack a heavy punch, so integrate them gingerly. Always taste your spice mixture and pickling liq uid before canning, and remember that flavors continue to age and marinate after the jars are sealed.

• Don't be afraid — pickles are one of the safest foods to can. They are protected from mold and bacteria growth due to high acidity levels in vinegar, and they won't explode during the canning process despite the water's high heat and pressure.

7 STEPS TO QUICK PICKLE ANY VEGETABLE

Pickles are a favorite with many people around the world, and just like anything else when it comes to food, nothing beats a homemade recipe. While the store-bought type of pickles are still a good choice for your home pantry and refrigerator, being able to pickle your own cucumbers is an extremely simple and delicious process. But you don't have to just limit your home pickling to cucumbers. In fact, just about any vegetable can be q uick pickled for a tasty treat – the sky's the limit with so many different options.

Professional and amateur chefs alike can make some q uality pickled vegetables. Almost any kind of veggie can be improved with the pickling process, ranging from okra, tomatillos, beets, to carrots. Plus they make for a great addition to any salad or just to snack on by themselves. No canning is req uired during the process either, which makes it even less of a hassle.

What is a Quick Pickle?

Quick pickles are produce that are soaked in brine in your refrigerator, as opposed to the outdoor fermented process. Even though the fermented kind is developed a little differently and has a deeper flavor, q uick pickled vegetables are enjoyable too. Vinegar, salt, sugar, water and spices are often used to make up the brine, and within just a few days they'll be ready to be served with a meal or eaten with a snack.

Fresh Is Best

For best pickling results, always use your freshest vegetables on hand. If they are starting to get a bit soft or bruised, save those for another dish such as your next soup or stew. You can use any vegetable that you want for a quick pickling, and they can all be carved into whatever shapes are desirable as well. For example, carrots are be sliced into thin sticks and cucumbers can be formed into medallions to fit into a glass jar along with the brine.

Brine Basics

A basic brine recipe includes equal parts of water and vinegar, and it can be adjusted to your preference of strong flavor. Any kind of vinegar is able to be used, including apple cider vinegar, white wine vinegar, rice vinegar, or any basic kind of vinegar. Try not to use either malt vinegar or balsamic vinegar though, as they are too concentrated and aged for good pickling results.

Quick Pickling Steps

Step 1: Prepare Your Vegetables

The first step to any cooking process is to wash and clean your vegetables, so that you can remove any grime or excess dirt on the outer layer of their skin. When it comes to pickling cucumbers, tomatillos, turnips, tomatoes, and other similar vegetables dice them up into whatever size and shape that you like. There are other vegetables that turn out much better if they are blanched, meaning briefly boiled so that they are just slightly soft. Vegetables that are recommended to be blanched include carrots, okra, green beans, peppers, ginger, beets, brussel sprouts, and others of that sort. If you decide that you want to go the blanching route, simply boil 16 cups of water for every pound of vegetables that you have and cook them at a boil for just two minutes. Be sure to cool them down in a bowl of ice water before putting them in your pickling jars.

Step 2: Prepare the Jars

For starters, get two wide mouth glass pint jars with lids and soak them in warm soapy water. Rinse them well and either dry them completely or set them aside to dry naturally. If you plan on pickling a lot of vegetables, more than two jars may be needed. Using clear glass jars is another useful tip, so that you can watch the status of your vegetables as they begin to pickle over the time in your refrigerator.

Step 3: Divide the Vegetables

After you've got your vegetables chopped, blanched, and sliced how you want, divide them up among how many jars you have set out and put them aside. In the end, you will want to make sure not to overfill the jars or pack the vegetables in there too tight, so that the liq uid has access to all of them. Getting a lot of veggies in one jar is perfectly fine, but after you are all done you can test the liq uid's ability to move around by shaking the jar. If all of the vegetable pieces move, you are good to go.

Step 4: Add Flavorings and Spices

This stage allows you to get your creative juices flowing, literally! There is no right or wrong combination of flavorings and spices, so think about which herbs appeal the most to your taste palate. Be bold and mix and match a lot of different spices to see what works best for you. Here are some general measurements to go by, that would be a decent amount per glass pint jar.

1/2 tsp. cumin seed

1/2 tsp turmeric

1/2 tsp dill seed

1/2 tsp mustard seed

1/2 tsp pickling spice

1 jalapeno pepper

1 sprig of fresh oregano

2-4 sprigs of fresh dill

These are just examples, but they are common ingredients that people like to add into their pickling jars. Other options might include black pepper, garlic salt, onion powder, or even coriander. Put your spice mixture into each jar before adding the vegetables.

Here are some additional flavorings that are suggested for a q uick pickling:

Fresh herbs: rosemary, thyme, savory

Dried herbs: rosemary, thyme, marjoram, oregano

Whole spices: mustard seed, peppercorns, red pepper flakes, bay leaves

Ground spices: smoked paprika, cajun seasoning, or cayenne pepper

Step 5: Make the Brine

Dry additions from your spice cabinet are great, but so are wet ingredients, such as minced garlic, diced jalapenos, or a teaspoon of horseradish. You can also tailor your brine to be sweet or tangy depending on what you mix together in your jars. Below are two examples of brine recipes, one that is appropriate for a sour flavor and another that is sweeter.

Sour Brine Recipe:

3 cups distilled apple cider vinegar (or white vinegar)

3 cups water

2 tsp of sea salt

2 tbsp sugar

Place all of the ingredients into a saucepan and bring to a boil until nothing is left undissolved. Let it boil for two minutes and then remove the pan from the heat.

Sweet Brine Recipe:

3 cups of distilled white vinegar or apple cider vinegar

3 cups water

1 1/2 cups plus 1 tbsp of sugar

1 tsp sea salt

Place all of these ingredients into a saucepan and then bring the mixture to a boil. As it heats up, be sure to keep stirring until all of the sugar and salt are dissolved. Bring to a boil for two minutes and then remove from heat.

After your brine is made, pour it into the jars and leave be sure to leave it within ½ inch from the top. It might be the case that you have more brine than you need, so be aware that not every single drop needs to be used.

Step 6: Remove Air Bubbles

After pouring your brine into the jars with the vegetables and flavorings, you may notice that some bubbles are forming on top. It's best to remove them as soon as possible, which can easily be done by tapping the jars against the counter a few times to get rid of them all. It might help to pour a little less brine than you initially need, so that once you remove all of the air bubbles you can top it off with a little more liq uid to smooth out the surface.

Step 7: Seal the Jars

After all your goods are tucked away in jars, seal them up and make sure that the vegetables are fully covered with the brine. Place your jars in the refrigerator for at least 24 hours before eating anything, however, if you q uick pickled okra or turnips they do better staying in the fridge for at least a week before serving. All the veggies are good for up to two months if they are kept in a cool place unless you decide to can them, which is not necessary for this process but can be done.

Tips for Giving your Homemade Pickled Vegetables Great Texture

Now that the basic recipe and method has been established, there are still a few extra things that you can do to ensure that your homemade pickles (and other vegetables) turn out to be the very best version of themselves. Sometimes the difference between a good pickle and a great pickle can be a matter of just a little bit extra effort. Here are some tips to make your q uick pickled items fantastic:

Pay Attention to the Size of your Chop

As you chop your vegetables, make sure you have an idea of what size and shape you want them to end up. That's because the more you work with them and chop them, the less crisp they become. You may want your pickles to be softer to compliment your burger or as a side salad, but in case you want that nice sharp crunch, be aware that they have to be a bit larger. This is why whole pickles are a lot firmer than butter pickles, as they were given a chance to stiffen up.

Trim the Blossom End from Your Cucumbers

Even though this tip is really only meant for cucumbers, it will make all the difference in the world for your homemade pickles from these juicy veggies. One of the best ways to immediately improve the texture of your cucumbers is to cut off their blossom ends. The reason for this is because this part of the cuke is where an enzyme is stored that can cause the vegetables to go limp. So, by cutting the end off right away you will soon notice how much better the texture of pickles will be.

Add in Some Onions for Extra Flavor

One vegetable that doesn't take up a lot of room, but adds a lot of flavor to the mix is an onion. Red, white, sweet, or yellow kinds all pickle really well and also enhances the other veggies in the jar with it. These can be an excellent addition to your next salad, coleslaw or summer barbecue, as the pickled onions would go delightfully on top of any burger or hot dog.

Throw in a Few Hard Boiled Eggs

Pickled veggies are great for snacking on, and adding some hard boiled eggs to your q uick pickled jar of goods might be a delicious way to enhance your serving tray. Eggs don't need any more time than regular cut vegetables to be pickled, and they are an equally healthy treat that are sure to impress anyone who stops by your home for a snack or dinner.

Before Making your Brine, Measure What You Need

There is nothing worse than making your brine and boiling it only to find that you haven't made nearly enough. To avoid short-changing yourself, measure how much liq uid you need with water before you get started so that you know what measurements to have. Since liq uids evaporate a little after being put on heat feel free to make much more brine than you thought you would need in the first place. It's better to have too much than too little.

Give Your Brine Some Time

Just because the recipe calls for your veggies to sit for 24 hours, doesn't mean that more time would hurt them. In fact, the longer that you allow your q uick pickled vegetables to sit, the better the flavor will be in the end. It might be a good idea to hide them from yourself in the back of the refrigerator, or put them in your second fridge for at least a week so that they become nice and marinated.

CHAPTER THREE

WHAT'S THE DIFFERENCE BETWEEN PICKLING AND FERMENTING?

You know you love all things pickled and fermented, but do you know the difference between the two? Both are processes of preservation that allow you to consume certain things long after their non-preserved counterparts, and both add a pleasant tanginess that can't be replicated any other way. Learn a few key distinctions and hit that jar of dilly beans or kimchi with more confidence than ever.

PICKLING

Pickling involves submerging anything edible and porous, such as vegetables and fruits, eggs, cheese, meat, poultry, and fish, in vinegar, salt or salt-and-sugar brine in order to preserve it. Pickled cheese, eh? Ever tried feta? It develops its signature tangy-saline flavor and slight funk from a quick aging in strong salt brine. And pickled eggs and pig bits in the American South, especially Louisiana, are pantry staples. You can pickle ingredients cooked or raw, depending on what they are (eggs and pig bits should be boiled beforehand, for example) or kick-start the process by pouring hot or warm brine over the material. This opens up its pores and allows the salty liq uid to start doing its thing, whereas brining in chilled liq uid allows vegetables to maintain their crisp texture and bright color.

The amounts of time they'll stay preserved depends on whether the pickles were refrigerated, prepared in sterilized jars and processed in a water bath or are simply more prone to spoilage. Suffice it to say, however, that they'll last longer than their non-pickled counterparts since brine is too acidic for harmful bacteria to thrive in.

FERMENTATION

Fermenting refers to the anaerobic sugar metabolization process carried out by yeast and bacteria in sealed containers of raw foods like cabbage (kimchi/sauerkraut), grapes (wine) and milk (yogurt). Unlike your compost heap, this method of organic decomposition results in carbon dioxide plus the natural preservatives of alcohol (in the case of wine) or lactic acid (vegetables), which transform the raw material into a nutritionally enhanced version. This process results in a signature tangy "fermented" flavor and pumped-up resistance to pathogens and spoilage. Ever wonder why your sourdough boule lasts longer than your supermarket loaf? Its dough, which is sour due to lactic acid, contains natural preservatives from fermentation.

Fermented foods stay fresh for a long time — up to a year or more — and in many cases are more delicious the more they're aged. Best of all, the microbes that help keep your internal flora healthy (probiotics) are hardy little things. Even if your kombucha loses its fizz, your yogurt is frozen into pops or your sauerkraut is braised, the probiotics will remain.

CHAPTER FOUR

PICKLED FOOD RECIPES

GARLIC DILL PICKLES RECIPE

YIELD: 10 to 12

ACTIVE TIME: 30 minutes

TOTAL TIME: 1 week

Ingredients

2 q uart kirby cucumbers (approximately 3 pounds)

1 1/2 cups apple cider vinegar

1 1/2 cups filtered water

2 tablespoons pickling salt

8 garlic cloves, peeled

4 teaspoons dill seed

2 teaspoons black peppercorns

1 teaspoon red chili flakes

Directions

1. Wash jars thoroughly in warm, soapy water. If you plan on making shelf stable pickles, prepare a boiling water bath canner. Put fresh canning jar lids into a small saucepan with 3 inches of water and set to the barest simmer.

2.Wash and dry kirby cucumbers. Remove blossom end. Cut into chips, spears or leave whole, depending on your preference.

3. Combine vinegar, water and salt in sauce pan and bring to a boil.

4. Eq ually divide garlic cloves, dill seed, black peppercorns and red chili flakes between jars. Pack prepared cucumbers into jars as tightly as you can without crushing them.

5. Pour the brine into the jars, leaving 1/4 inch headspace (that's the amount of space between the surface of the brine and the rim of the jar).

6. Remove any air bubbles from jars by gently tapping them. You can also use a wooden chopstick or plastic utensil to help remove stubborn bubbles.

7. Wipe rims and apply lids and bands (don't screw them on too tightly).

8. If processing jars for shelf stability, lower jars into your processing pot. When water returns to a boil, set a timer for 10 minutes.

9. When time is up, remove jars from canning pot and allow them to cool. When jars are cool enough to handle, check seals.

10. If you choose not to process your jars, let them cool before putting them into the refrigerator. Do note that your jars may seal during the cooling process. However, without the boiling water bath process, that doesn't mean they're shelf stable. Still refrigerate.

11. Let pickles rest for at least one week before eating.

MARINATED FAVA BEANS RECIPE

Makes 1 cup

Active time: 45 minutes

Total time: 1 hour

Ingredients

1 1/2 pounds fava beans (or 3/4 cup frozen beans)

2 tablespoons sherry or red wine vinegar

2 tablespoons olive oil

1 medium garlic clove, finely minced (about 1 teaspoon)

2 sprigs fresh rosemary

1/2 teaspoon salt

1/4 teaspoon freshly ground black pepper

Directions

1. Bring a pot of salted water to a boil. While the water heats, remove the fava beans from their long pods. Once the water boils, add the fava beans and cook until bright green and just tender, about 3 minutes. Drain and immediately rinse under cold water. Pop the bright green fava beans out of their casing and set aside.

2. In a pint jar, combine the vinegar, olive oil, garlic, rosemary sprigs, salt, and pepper. Place a lid on the jar and shake to combine the vinaigrette.Pour prepared fava beans

into the jar of vinaigrette. Replace lid and shake to coat the fava beans.

3. Let stand at least 15 minutes before serving. Marinated fava beans will last 2-3 days in the refrigerator.

PICKLED OYSTER MUSHROOMS RECIPE

Yield: 2 pints

Active time: 45 minutes

Total time: 48 hours

Ingredients

1 pound oyster mushrooms

2 1/2 cups rice vinegar

1 small onion, sliced

1 tablespoon pickling salt

1 tablespoon sugar

1/4 teaspoon black peppercorns

2 bay leaves

2 garlic cloves, peeled and sliced

Directions

1) Wash oyster mushrooms well and chop them into pieces.

2) Bring a pot of salted water to a boil and simmer the oyster mushrooms for 8-10 minutes, until they're tender.

3) In a medium pot, combine vinegar, onion, salt, sugar and peppercorns. Bring to a boil.

4) When the oyster mushrooms are tender, drain them well and transfer them to the brine.

5) Cook mushrooms in brine for 5 minutes.

6) Divide bay leaves and garlic between two prepared pint jars.

7) Pack oyster mushrooms and onions into jars and top with brine, leaving 1/2 inch headspace.

8) Use a wooden spoon or chopstick to remove air bubbles from jars. If necessary, add more brine to return the headspace to 1/2 inch.

9) Wipe rims, apply lids and rings and process jars in a boiling water bath for 15 minutes.

10) When time is up, remove jars from canning pot and let jars cool on a folded kitchen towel.

11) When jars are cool, check lids to ensure a good seal. Any unsealed jars should be stored in the refrigerator.

12) Let pickles rest at least 48 hours before opening.

13) Sealed pickles are shelf stable for up to one year.

LEMONY PICKLED CAULIFLOWER RECIPE

Yield: MAKES 1 q uart

Active Time: 15 minutes

Total Time: 12 hours

Ingredients

2 pounds cauliflower

1 cup apple cider vinegar

1 cup water

2 teaspoons sea salt

1 small lemon, sliced

1 large garlic clove, sliced

1/4 teaspoon peppercorns

Directions

1) Wash cauliflower and break it into florets.

2) In a large saucepan, combine the apple cider vinegar, water and sea salt. Bring to a boil.

3) Place two slices of lemon in the bottom of a q uart jar and top with garlic clove slices and peppercorns. Set aside.

4) When brine is boiling, add cauliflower to the pot. Stir until the brine returns to a boil and remove from heat.

5) Using tongs pack cauliflower into the prepared jar and top with brine.

6) Place 2-3 slices of lemon on top of the cauliflower and put a lid on the jar.

7) Let pickles sit out on counter until cool. Once they've reached room temperature, refrigerate jar.

8) Pickles are ready to eat within 12 hours, though they will continue to deepen in flavor the longer the rest.

QUICK PICKLED FENNEL WITH ORANGE RECIPE

Yield: makes 1 quart

Active time: 20 minutes

Total time: 24 hours

Ingredients

3 small fennel bulbs

2 tablespoons kosher salt

1 small orange, sliced

1/4 teaspoon freshly ground black pepper

1 cup apple cider vinegar

Directions

1) Wash fennel bulbs and remove stems. Slice in half and cut out the hard core.

2) Slice paper-thin on a mandoline.

3) Sprinkle kosher salt over shaved fennel and toss to combine. Let fennel sit for at least an hour.

4) When time is up, pour fennel into a colander and sq ueeze to remove the liq uid that was produced while it sat with the salt.

5) Return fennel to the bowl and toss with orange slices and black pepper.

6) Pack fennel and orange into a q uart jar and top with the apple cider vinegar.

7) Use a chopstick or the end of a wooden spoon to work the vinegar down into the fennel.

8) Stash jar in the fridge and let sit for at least 24 hours before eating.

9) This q uick pickle will keep at least 2-3 weeks in the refrigerator.

RED BEET EGGS RECIPE

Yield: makes 1 quart

Active Time: 20 minutes

Total Time: 48 hours

Ingredients

8 hardboiled eggs, peeled

1 cup canned pickle red beets (with their liquid)

1/2 cup apple cider vinegar

1/2 cup water

2 tablespoons brown sugar

1 cinnamon stick

4 cloves

Directions

1) Place peeled hard boiled eggs in a quart-sized mason jar (or any other heatproof container of similar size).

2) In a medium saucepan, combine pickled beets, apple cider vinegar, water and brown sugar. Heat until it just comes to a boil.

3) Place the cinnamon sticks and cloves into the jar with the eggs. Carefully pour the pickling liquid and beet slices into the jar with the eggs. Tap the jar to help loosen any air bubbles. Use a long, skinny spatula to ease out any remaining air bubbles. Place a lid on the jar. Once it has

cooled to room temperature, refrigerate. Let pickles rest at least 48 hours before eating.

BREAD AND BUTTER PICKLES RECIPE

Yield: makes 2 pints

Active time: 1 hour

Total time: 48 hours

Ingredients

4 cups thickly sliced pickling cucumbers (8 to 10 pickling cucumbers)

1 cup sliced red bell peppers (about 1 small)

1 cup sliced onion (about 1 medium)

2 tablespoons pickling salt

1 cup apple cider vinegar

3/4 cup granulated sugar

1 tablespoon mustard seed

1 teaspoon celery seed

1/2 teaspoon red pepper flakes

1/4 teaspoon ground cloves

Directions

1) Prepare two pint jars and a small canning pot. Combine the sliced cucumbers, bell peppers, onion, and pickling salt in a colander set in a large bowl. Refrigerate for one hour to remove excess liq uid. Rinse vegetables and discard liquid.

2) Combine the vinegar and sugar in a large pot. Heat over medium heat until the sugar is dissolved. Add the mustard

seed, celery seed, red pepper flakes and cloves. Increase the heat to high and bring the brine to a boil.

3) Add the drained vegetables and stir to combine. Cook for 5 minutes, until all the vegetables in the brine are fully heated through. Using tongs, fill the sterilized jars with the vegetables. Slowly pour the hot brine over the vegetables in each jar, leaving 1/2 inch headspace.

4) Gently tap the jars on a towel-lined countertop to help loosen any bubbles before using a wooden chopstick to dislodge any remaining bubbles. Check the headspace again and add more brine if necessary.

5) Wipe the rims, apply the lids and rings, and process in a hot water bath for 10 minutes. Let these pickles cure for at least 48 hours before eating.

SWEET AND SPICY PICKLE RELISH RECIPE

Yield: makes 2 pints

Active time: 45 minutes

Total time: 1 hour

Ingredients

3 cups grated green pepper (about 2 large)

3 cups grated pickling cucumber (6 to 8 pickles)

1 cup minced or grated onion (about 1 medium)

2 cups apple cider vinegar, divided

1 cup granulated sugar

1 tablespoon kosher salt

1 tablespoon mustard seed

1/2 teaspoon celery seed

1 teaspoon red chili flakes

Directions

1) Combine prepared green pepper, cucumber, and onion in a large, non-reactive (stainless steel or enamel-coated) pot. Stir in one cup of apple cider vinegar and bring to a simmer. Simmer, stirring occasionally, until the vegetables have cooked down and the liq uid is reduced by about 1/3, about 30 minutes. Drain the vegetables, discard liq uid, and return vegetables to the pot.

2) Add remaining vinegar, sugar and the spices. Bring to a simmer and cook for five minutes. Remove pot from heat.

3) Fill jars, wipe rims, apply lids and rings. Process in a boiling water canner for 10 minutes (starting time when pot returns to a boil). Remove jars from pot and let cool on a towel-lined countertop.

4) When jars are completely cool, remove the rings and test the seals. The relish is good to eat immediately. Store sealed jars in a cool dark place for up to a year.

PICKLED GARLIC RECIPE

Yield: makes 3 half pint jars

Active time:45 minutes

Total time: 48 hours

Ingredients

1 pound fresh garlic, peeled

1 cup red wine vinegar

1 cup water

1 tablespoon pickling salt

Directions

1) Prepare a small canning pot and 3 half pint jars. Place 3 new lids in a small pot of water and bring to the barest simmer.

2) Combine vinegar, water and salt in a saucepan and bring to a boil.

3) Pack garlic cloves into prepared jars.

4) Pour hot brine over the garlic cloves.

5) Tap jars gently to remove any trapped air bubbles. If necessary, add more brine to return the headspace to 1/2 inch.

6) Wipe rims, apply lids and rings and process jars in a boiling water bath canner for 10 minutes (start your timer when the water returns to a boil, not when the jars first go in).

7) When time is up, remove jars from canner and let cool on a folded kitchen towel.

8) When jars are cool enough to handle, remove rings and test seals by grasping edges of lids and carefully lifting jars. If lids hold fast, seals are good.

9) Store jars in a cool, dark place. They are ready to eat within 48 hours, but can be kept up to one year.

PICKLED BRUSSELS SPROUT HALVES RECIPE

Yield: 2 pints

Active time: 25 minutes

Total time: 48 hours

Ingredients

1 pound Brussels sprouts

1 1/2 cups apple cider vinegar

1 cup water

1 tablespoon pickling salt

20 peppercorns, divided

1/4 teaspoon yellow mustard seeds, divided

2 garlic cloves

2 bay leaves

Directions

1) Trim the sprouts and cut them in half. Set aside.

2) Combine vinegar, water and salt in a non-reactive pot and bring to a boil.

3) Divide the peppercorns, mustard seeds, garlic cloves and bay leaves between 2 prepared pint jars.

4) Pack sprouts into jars.

5) Pour brine over the sprouts.

6) Use a wooden chopstick to remove air bubbles from jars.

7) Wipe rims, apply lids and rings and process in a boiling water bath for 10 minutes.

8) When time is up, remove jars from canner and let cool on a folded towel.

9) When jars are cool, test seals. If seals are good, jars can be stored in pantry (any unsealed jars should be refrigerated). Give pickles at least 48 hours before you eat them, so that the brine fully penetrates the veg.

10) Sealed jars will keep up to one year on the pantry shelf.

MARINATED CARROTS WITH MINT RECIPE

Yield: 4

Active time: 15 minutes

Total time: 1 hour

Ingredients

1 1/2 pounds carrots

1/4 cup olive oil

3 tablespoons seasoned rice vinegar

2 tablespoons chopped mint

1 small clove garlic, minced

1/2 teaspoon sea salt

1/4 teaspoon freshly ground black pepper

Directions

1) Peel carrots and slice them into thick rounds. Simmer in a pot of salted water until just tender.

2) While carrots cook, whisk together olive oil, vinegar, mint, garlic, salt and pepper.

3) When carrots are fork tender, drain them.

4) Toss warm carrots together with vinaigrette and let them sit until carrots are cool.

5) Place carrots in refrigerator and let them marinate for at least 1 hour before serving. They can be kept in the refrigerator for up to 5 days.

SHREDDED KOHLRABI QUICK PICKLE RECIPE

Yield: Makes 2 quarts

Active Time: 20 minutes

Total Time: 2 hours

Ingredients

2 pounds kohlrabi

2 cups red wine vinegar

2 cups water

2 tablespoons honey

2 tablespoons pickling salt

1 tablespoon grated fresh ginger

1 garlic clove, grated

1/2 teaspoon black peppercorns

1/4 red chili flakes

Directions

1) Wash and dry two quart jars. Set aside.

2) Clean and trim kohlrabi bulbs. Using a mandoline slicer or a food processor, slice kohlrabi into thin sticks.

3) Divide the shreds evenly between the two jars.

4) Combine vinegar, water, honey, pickling salt, ginger, garlic, black peppercorns and red chili flakes in a medium saucepan and bring to a boil.

5) Once brine is boiling vigorously, remove it from the heat and carefully pour the brine over the kohlrabi.

6) Place lids on the jars and let them sit until cool.

7) Once jars are cool to the touch, refrigerate the pickles and eat with salads, sandwiches or meat dishes.

PICKLED EGGPLANT WITH MINT AND GARLIC RECIPE

Yield: makes 2 pints

Ingredients

2 1/2 cups red wine vinegar

1 1/2 pounds eggplant, peeled and cut into 1/2 inch cubes

1 1/2 tablespoons chopped garlic

1/4 cup mint leaves

1 1/2 teaspoons pickling salt

Directions

1) Prepare a small canning pot and 2 pint jars. Place 2 new lids in a small pot of water and bring to the barest simmer.

2) Pour vinegar into a medium saucepan and bring to a boil. Once it boils, add eggplant and simmer for 2-3 minutes.

3) When time is up, remove eggplant cubes from vinegar with a slotted spoon and place them in a bowl. Add garlic, mint and salt and stir to combine.

4) Pack eggplant into jars and top with boiling vinegar, leaving 1/2 inch headspace.

5) Tap jars gently to remove any trapped air bubbles. If necessary, add more brine to return the headspace to 1/2 inch.

6) Wipe rims, apply lids and rings and process jars in a boiling water bath canner for 10 minutes (start your timer

when the water returns to a boil, not when the jars first go in).

7) When time is up, remove jars from canner and let cool on a folded kitchen towel.

8) When jars are cool enough to handle, remove rings and test seals by grasping edges of lids and carefully lifting jars. If lids hold fast, seals are good.

9) Store jars in a cool, dark place. They are ready to eat within 1 week, but can be kept up to one year.

SPICY DILLY BEANS RECIPE

Yield: makes 5 pints

Active time: 1 hour

Total time: 1 week

Ingredients

3 pounds green beans

2 1/2 cups white vinegar

2 1/2 cups water

4 tablespoons pickling salt

5 medium cloves garlic

5 teaspoons dill seed (not dill weed)

5 teaspoons red chili flakes

Directions

1) Prepare a boiling water bath and 5 regular mouth pint jars. Place lids in a small saucepan over very low heat to simmer while you prepare the pickles.

2) Wash and trim beans so that they fit in jar. If you have particularly long beans, cut them in half. Combine vinegar, water and salt in a medium saucepan and bring to a boil. While the pickling liquid heats, pack your beans into the jars, leaving 1/2 inch for headspace. To each jar, add 1 clove of garlic, 1 teaspoon dill seeds, and 1 teaspoon red chili flakes.

3) Slowly pour the hot brine over the beans, leaving 1/2 inch for headspace. After all the jars are full, use a wooden

chopstick to work the air bubbles out of the jars. Check the headspace again and add more brine if necessary.

4) Wipe the rims, apply lids and rings and process in a hot water bath for 10 minutes. Let pickles sit for at least one week before eating.

PICKLED SECKEL PEARS RECIPE

Yield: makes 2 pints

Active time: 45 minutes

Total time: 48 hours

Ingredients

1 1/2 pounds Seckel pears

1 cup apple cider vinegar

1/3 cup granulated white sugar

1 teaspoon pickling salt

1 cinnamon stick, broken in half

6 cloves

Directions

1) Prepare a small boiling water bath canner and two regular mouth pint jars. Place lids in a small saucepan and bring to a low simmer.

2) Wash Seckel pears. Cut into halves and remove seeds (a small melon baller does this task well).

3) Combine apple cider vinegar, granulated sugar and salt with 1 cup water and bring to a boil.

4) Divide cinnamon stick halves and cloves between the two pint jars.

5) Tightly pack pear halves into the jars, cut-side down.

6) Pour hot brine over pear halves, leaving 1/2 inch headspace. Tap jars to remove any trapped bubbles and adjust brine levels, if necessary.

7) Wipe rims, apply lids and bands and process jars in a boiling water bath canner for 15 minutes.

8) When time is up, remove jars from canner and let cool on a folded kitchen towel. When jars are cool, remove bands and test seals. Wash jars to remove any stickiness.

9) Any unsealed jars should be refrigerated. Sealed jars can be safely stored in a cool, dark place for up to 1 year.

10) Let these pickled pears sit for at least 48 hours before eating, to allow pickle flavor to fully infuse.

PICKLED PRUNES RECIPE

Yield: makes 1 generous pint

Active time: 30 minutes

Total time: 60 minutes

Ingredients

1 pound pitted prunes

1 cup red wine vinegar

1 small blood orange, zest removed with peeler

1/4 cup brown sugar

1/4 cup honey

1 teaspoon grated fresh ginger

1/4 teaspoon black peppercorns

1/4 teaspoon whole cloves

1/8 teaspoon red chili flakes

4 green cardamom pods

3 allspice berries

1 star anise

1 bay leaf

pinch sea salt

Directions

1) Combine prunes and red wine vinegar in a medium saucepan.

2) Add strips of blood orange zest and juice the fruit into the pan.

3) Add the rest of the ingredients and bring to a simmer.

4) Cook for 15-20 minutes, until the prunes have plumped and the liq uid has reduced to a thin syrup.

5) Remove pan from heat and let prunes cool a little.

6) Spoon into a jar and refrigerate. Pickled prunes will keep in the fridge for up to one month.

SWEET PICKLED DAIKON RADISH RECIPE

Yield: makes 2 pints

Active time: 30 minutes

Total time: 48 hours

Ingredients

1 pound daikon radish

1 1/2 cups rice wine vinegar

1/2 cup water

1/2 cup sugar

1 tablespoon pickling salt

1/2 teaspoon black pepper corns

Directions

1) Prepare a small canning pot and 2 pint jars. Place 2 new lids in a small pot of water and bring to the barest simmer.

2) Slice daikon into thin rounds using a mandoline, food processor or knife. Keep the slices around 1/4 inch thick so that they retain some crunch.

3) Combine rice wine vinegar, water, sugar and salt in a medium saucepan and bring to a boil.

4) Divide peppercorns between your two jars.

5) Pack daikon slices into jars. One pound should fit perfectly into two pint jars. Top with boiling brine, leaving 1/2 inch headspace.

6) Tap jars gently to remove any trapped air bubbles. If necessary, add more brine to return the headspace to 1/2 inch.

7) Wipe rims, apply lids and rings and process jars in a boiling water bath canner for 10 minutes (start your timer when the water returns to a boil, not when the jars first go in).

8) When time is up, remove jars from canner and let cool on a folded kitchen towel.

9) When jars are cool enough to handle, remove rings and test seals by grasping edges of lids and carefully lifting jars. If lids hold fast, seals are good.

10) Store jars in a cool, dark place. They are ready to eat within 48 hours, but can be kept up to one year.

PICKLED CHINESE LONG BEANS RECIPE

Yield: makes 2 pints

Active time: 30 minutes

Total time: 2 weeks

Ingredients

2 pounds Chinese long beans

1 cup white vinegar

1 tablespoon pickling salt

6 garlic cloves

2 bay leaves

2 star anise

1 teaspoon black peppercorns

1/2 teaspoon red pepper flakes

Directions

1) Prepare a boiling water bath canner and 2 wide mouth pint jars. Place lids in a small saucepan, cover them with water, and simmer over very low heat.

2) Wash and trim beans.

3) Combine vinegar with pickling salt and 1 cup water in small pot and bring to a simmer.

4) Divide garlic and spices between to the two pint jars.

5) Spiral the beans into the jars, packing them in as tightly as possible.

6) Pour brine over the beans. Gently tap jars to remove any trapped air bubbles and add more brine, if necessary.

7) Wipe rims, apply lids and rings and process in a hot water bath for 10 minutes.

8) When time is up, remove jars from canner and let cool. Check lids ensure a seal.

9) Let jars sit for at least 2 weeks before eating, to ensure sufficiently pickling.

PICKLED HAKUREI TURNIPS RECIPE

Yield: makes 1 pint

Active time: 10 minutes

Total time: 1 hour

Ingredients

1 bunch hakurei turnips (approximately six, see note above)

1 teaspoon salt

1/2 cup rice wine vinegar

1 teaspoon sugar

1/2 tea black peppercorns, crushed

3 thin slices of ginger

Directions

1) Wash turnips well and slice them thinly on a mandolin. Place turnip slices in a small bowl and toss with the salt. Let rest until there is a pool of liq uid on the bottom of the bowl, about 30 minutes. Drain turnips of the salty water and pack into a pint sized mason jar.

2) Add vinegar, sugar, pepper and ginger slices. Apply a watertight lid and shake to combine. Place pickled turnips in the fridge and chill before eating. Pickles can be eaten within an hour of being made and will keep for at least a week.

PICKLED RED TOMATOES RECIPE

Yield: makes 3 pints

Active time: 45 minutes

Total time: 1 week

Ingredients

2 pounds small, meaty tomatoes, peeled (like roma, plum or San Marzano)

1 1/2 cups red wine vinegar

2 tablespoons pickling salt

3/4 cup granulated sugar

2-inch piece fresh ginger, thinly sliced

3 tablespoons pickling spice

Directions

1) If canning, prepare a boiling water bath canner and 3 regular mouth pint jars. Place lids in a small saucepan, cover them with water, and simmer over very low heat.

2) Combine vinegar, 1 1/2 cups of water, salt, sugar, and ginger slices in a pot and bring to a boil.

3) Line up jars and measure 1 tablespoon of pickling spices into the bottom of each jar.

4) Carefully pack peeled tomatoes into prepared jars, taking care not to crush them.

5) Slowly pour brine over the tomatoes, leaving 1/2 inch headspace.

6) Gently tap jars on a towel-lined countertop to help loosen any air bubbles. Use a wooden chopstick or plastic knife to help remove any bubbles that remain after tapping.

7) Check headspace again and add more brine if necessary. Make sure to include 2 to 3 ginger slices per jar.

8) Wipe rims, apply lids and rings and process in a hot water bath for 10 minutes.

9) If you're skipping the processing step, simply let jars cool on your countertop after capping. Once they reach room temperature, put them into the refrigerator.

10) Whether you process these pickles or not, let them rest in the brine for at least a week before eating.

CHAPTER FIVE

FERMENTED PICKLE RECIPES

LACTO-FERMENTED "KOSHER" DILL PICKLES

Ingredients:

5 Tbsp. sea salt

2 q uarts chlorine-free water

4-6 grape, oak, or horseradish leaves

6-9 cloves garlic, peeled

2 large heads of dill

Spices to taste: black peppercorns, red pepper flakes, mustard seeds, etc. (Secret ingredient: for an extra bite, add a few strips of fresh horseradish to the spice mix!)

Enough pickling cucumbers to fill a ½-gallon jar

Instructions:

Make brine by dissolving 5 tablespoons sea salt in 2 quarts of chlorine-free water.

In a half-gallon jar add a couple of the tannin-containing leaves, a few cloves of garlic, the heads of dill, and of the spices.

Pack half of the cucumbers tightly on top of the spices. (The longest ones work best at the bottom.)

Repeat a layer of leaves, garlic, and spices. Add another tightly packed layer of cucumbers and top them off with more garlic and spices.

Pour the brine over the pickles, leaving 1-2 inches of headspace. Place another tannin-containing leaf on top of the pickles as a cover between the pickles and the surface of the brine. Use a fermentation weight to keep the pickles under the liq uid, if necessary. Cover the jar with a tight lid, airlock lid, or coffee filter secured with a rubber band.

Ferment at room temperature (60-70°F is preferred) until desired flavor and texture are achieved. If using a tight lid, burp daily to release excess pressure. The brine should turn cloudy and bubbly, and the pickles should taste sour when done.

Eat right away, or store in a refrigerator or root cellar for months and enjoy them all winter long.

LACTO-FERMENTED KOHLRABI PICKLES WITH DILL AND MUSTARD

Ingredients:

1 handful of fresh dill

1½ tsp. of mustard seed

2 Tbsp. sea salt

1½-2 cups of water, as needed

3 medium kohlrabi, peeled and cut into spears

Instructions:

Place fresh dill and mustard seed in the bottom of a quart jar.

Combine water and salt; stir to dissolve.

Pack kohlrabi spears on top of the herbs and spices, leaving 1½ inches headspace.

Cover vegetables with brine, adding more water as needed to cover, but leaving 1 inch headspace.

If necessary, weigh the vegetables down under the brine.

Cover each jar with a tight lid, airlock lid, or coffee filter secured with a rubber band.

Culture at room temperature (60-70°F is preferred) until desired flavor and texture are achieved. If using a tight lid, burp daily to release excess pressure.

Once the vegetables are finished, put a tight lid on the jar and move to cold storage. The flavor will continue to develop.

LACTO-FERMENTED DILLY BEANS

Ingredients:

2 quarts water

4-6 Tbsp. sea salt

1 pound young green beans, trimmed

2 Tbsp. red pepper flakes, or to taste

4 garlic cloves, peeled and smashed

1 tsp. black peppercorns

2 large handfuls of dill (flowering heads preferred, but leaves work well too)

Instructions:

Dissolve sea salt in water to make brine. Set aside.

Divide the red pepper flakes, garlic cloves, peppercorns, and dill between 2 quart-size glass jars.

Place the green beans on top of the seasonings; straight up if they are long and thin or sideways if thicker and cut into chunks. Cover with brine solution, leaving 1 inch headspace at the top of jar

Cover the jar with a tight lid, airlock lid, or coffee filter secured with a rubber band.

Culture at room temperature (60-70°F is preferred) until desired flavor and texture are achieved. If using a tight lid, burp daily to release excess pressure.

Once the beans are finished, put a tight lid on the jar and move to cold storage.

LACTO-FERMENTED SLICED JALAPEÑOS

Ingredients:

1 pound whole green jalapeños, washed, tops cut off, cut horizontally into rounds.

4 to 5 clean pint jars, with lids and bands, sterilized and drained

Medium fermenting brine (about 1-1/2 Tbsp. salt in a quart of water)

Kombucha or raw apple cider vinegar

Instructions:

Clean 4 or 5 pint jars and rinse thoroughly.

Fill the jars with peppers, up to 1-1/2 inches below the rim of the jar. Wipe the rims of all the jars with a paper towel.

Pour 1 Tbsp. of the kombucha or vinegar into each jar. Fill the remaining space in the jars with the brine, coming up to 1 inch away from the rims.

Screw the lids and bands onto the filled jars, and set them in a cool place away from drafts and direct sunlight. Burp them once a day for the first week, once every other day for the second week, then once at the end of the third week.

Once they have reached your preferred level of fermentation, screw the lids on tightly and place the jars into a root cellar or refrigerator until you are ready to use them.

FERMENTED MOROCCAN-SPICED CARROTS

Ingredients:

4 cups grated carrots, tightly packed

2 cloves garlic, minced

1/2 cup cilantro, chopped

1 tsp. ground cumin

1/2 tsp. ground cinnamon

1 Tbsp. lemon juice

1 Tbsp. sea salt

INSTRUCTIONS:

Mix all ingredients and knead with clean hands or pound with a Cabbage Crusher to release juices.

Transfer the mixture to a glass jar, pressing to submerge completely underneath the liq uid. If necessary, use a fermentation weight to keep the vegetables under the liq uid.

Cover the jar with a tight lid, airlock lid, or coffee filter secured with a rubber band.

Culture at room temperature (60-70°F is preferred) until desired flavor and texture are achieved. If using a tight lid, burp daily to release excess pressure.

Once the carrots are finished, put a tight lid on the jar and move to cold storage. The flavor will continue to develop as it ages.

LACTO-FERMENTED SPICY SUMMER SQUASH RELISH

INGREDIENTS:

3-1/2 cups summer squash, shredded

1/2 cup onion, chopped

1 jalapeño pepper, seeded and chopped

1 medium bell pepper, chopped fine

3 cloves garlic, peeled and minced

1/4 tsp. red pepper flakes

1/2 Tbsp. sea salt

1/4 cup filtered water

2 small sprigs fresh dill

1/2 grape leaf

Black peppercorns, ground coarse

INSTRUCTIONS:

In a medium bowl, mix together the shredded squash, onion, jalapeño pepper, bell pepper, garlic, red pepper flakes, water and salt. Stir and crush slightly with a wooden spoon or Cabbage Crusher.

Pack the relish mixture into a jar, quart-sized or larger, pressing down to 1 inch below the rim of the jar. Add the dill and grape leaf, sliding them in against the side of the jar. Cover the jar with an airlock lid or regular lid.

Set the jar out at room temperature for 2-3 days.

Transfer jar to cold storage. Will keep for 2-3 weeks in the refrigerator.

LACTO-FERMENTED CUCUMBER RELISH

INGREDIENTS:

3 cups shredded cucumbers

2 red bell peppers, seeded and chopped

1 small onion, diced

Dill seed

Mustard seed

2-3 Tbsp. sea salt

1 quart filtered water

INSTRUCTIONS:

Sanitize one quart jar, with an airlock lid or standard ring-and-band.

In a large bowl, combine the cucumbers, peppers, and onion. Toss to combine.

Add 1 tsp. of dill seed, and 1/2 tsp. mustard seed. Stir with a wooden spoon.

Allow the vegetable mixture to sit, covered, on the kitchen counter for 30 minutes to let the juices combine a little.

Meanwhile, make light brine using the filtered water and sea salt, and chill it.

Begin filling the quart jar with the relish, pounding it down a bit to get the juices together and to get it to fit into the jar. Fill only to 1 inch below the rim of the jar.

Fill the jar with the light brine, using a butter knife to release any air bubbles caught against the side of the jar.

Screw down the lid of the jar and set it somewhere away from drafts and direct sunlight. Let it sit for 3 to 4 days, or until it becomes bubbly and fragrant.

Place the jar in the refrigerator until you are ready to use it.

LACTO-FERMENTED GRATED GINGER CARROTS

INGREDIENTS:

4 cups coarsely grated carrots

1 Tbsp. fresh grated ginger root

1 Tbsp. sea salt

INSTRUCTIONS:

In a medium bowl, mix carrots, ginger, and sea salt. Knead with clean hands or use a Cabbage Crusher until there is enough liquid to cover.

Transfer the mixture to a quart glass jar, pressing to submerge completely underneath the liquid. If necessary, add a bit of water to completely cover the mixture or use a fermentation weight to keep the vegetables under the liquid.

Cover the jar with a tight lid, airlock lid, or coffee filter secured with a rubber band.

Culture at room temperature (60-70°F is preferred) until desired flavor and texture are achieved. If using a tight lid, burp daily to release excess pressure.

Once the carrots are finished, put a tight lid on the jar and move to cold storage. The flavor will continue to develop as it ages.

LACTO-FERMENTED HABAÑERO GARLIC HOT SAUCE

INGREDIENTS:

5 lbs. organic habañeros

1 large whole head of garlic

5 Tbsp. sea salt

INSTRUCTIONS:

Remove the stems from the habañeros.

Peel, crush, and chop the garlic.

Use a food processor or blender to process the habañeros and garlic together into a paste. Add the salt and mix to thoroughly combine it into the habañero and garlic paste.

Place the mixture in an airlock fermentation set up and allow it to ferment for 6 weeks.

Once the fermented mixture has reached the taste profile you desire, you can add a bit of vinegar (such as raw apple cider vinegar) to further acidify.

LACTO-FERMENTED GARLIC CLOVES

INGREDIENTS:

12-14 heads of garlic

Brine of 1 q uart water + 2 Tbsp. sea salt

Herbs such as basil or oregano if desired

INSTRUCTIONS:

Peel garlic as indicated above. Fill a quart jar within 1 inch of the top with the garlic cloves.

Pour brine and herbs over garlic cloves.

Allow to ferment for 3 to 4 weeks before moving to cold storage. The longer these sit in cold storage the more delicious they get!

LACTO-FERMENTED CARROT AND PARSNIP PICKLES

INGREDIENTS:

1 pound parsnips

1 pound carrots

1 tsp. fresh grated ginger

1/4 tsp. red pepper flakes

2 Tbsp. sea salt

4 cups water

INSTRUCTIONS:

Wash parsnips and carrots well. Remove tops and cut lengthwise into small sticks. Cutting the sticks tall enough to fill jar 1 1/2 inches below the rim is helpful for even packing.

Place grated ginger and red pepper flakes in the bottom of a q uart jar. Place parsnip and carrot sticks atop ginger and red pepper flakes, trying to line them up and pack them in as evenly as possible. Leave 1 inch of headspace at the top of the jar.

Make a brine of 4 cups water to 2 Tbsp. sea salt. Stir to dissolve salt and pour over vegetables, leaving 1 inch of headspace.

Place the lid on the jar or add the airlock, if using. Ferment at room temperature 5-10 days. If not using an airlock, burp the jars daily to release the fermentation gases.

Once the initial fermentation period is over, and the carrots and parsnips are as tangy as desired, move jar to cold storage.

LACTO-FERMENTED WATERMELON RIND PICKLES

INGREDIENTS:

Rind from one or more watermelons

Sea salt

Filtered water

Spices as desired

INSTRUCTIONS:

Scrape the pink flesh from the watermelon rind. Peel the outer green skin from the watermelon rind. Cut the watermelon rind into 1-inch sq uares.

Prepare a light brine by combining 1-3 Tbsp. of salt and 1 q uart of filtered water.

Place watermelon rind squares and any spices you desire into a fermentation vessel. Fill up the remaining space in the jar with the salt solution. Use a wooden or plastic utensil to release any air bubbles trapped along the sides of the jar.

If necessary, weigh the rind pieces down under the brine.

Cover each jar with a tight lid, airlock lid, or coffee filter secured with a rubber band.

Culture at room temperature (60-70°F is preferred) until desired flavor and texture are achieved. If using a tight lid, burp daily to release excess pressure.

Once the culture is finished, put a tight lid on the jar and move to cold storage. The flavor will continue to develop.

LACTO-FERMENTED PINEAPPLE SALSA

INGREDIENTS:

1 pineapple

1 bunch cilantro

4 green onions

1 red jalapeno, seeded

2 tsp. sea salt

¼ cup whey or water kefir

½ cup water

INSTRUCTIONS:

Peel and core the pineapple. Dice into ¼-inch pieces and add to a medium-size bowl.

Mince the cilantro, green onions, and jalapeño; add to the pineapple.

Mix in sea salt, whey or water kefir, and water.

Transfer to a quart-size fermentation vessel. The brine should come at least 1 inch above the level of the pineapple mixture. If it doesn't, weigh the pieces of fruit and vegetables down with glass weights or another clean object. Seal the jar with an airtight lid or a lid with an airlock system. If using canning jar lids, be sure to burp the jars as needed during fermentation.

Ferment 2 to 4 days at room temperature or until bubbly and fermented to your taste before transferring to cold storage.

NATURALLY FERMENTED CARROT STICKS

INGREDIENTS:

1 q uart water

1-3 Tbsp. sea salt

2-3 pounds carrots, cut into sticks

INSTRUCTIONS:

Dissolve salt in water.

Place the carrot sticks in the jar and pour the liq uid over the carrots, leaving 1-2 inches headspace.

If necessary, weigh the carrots down under the brine to keep them submerged.

Cover the jar with a tight lid, airlock lid, or coffee filter secured with a rubber band.

Culture at room temperature (60-70°F is preferred) until desired flavor and texture are achieved. If using a tight lid, burp daily to release excess pressure.

Once the carrots are finished, put a tight lid on the jar and move to cold storage. The flavor will continue to develop as the carrots age.

LACTO-FERMENTED RADISHES

INGREDIENTS:

4 cups water

2-3 Tbsp. sea salt

2 bunches of radishes

Seasoning seeds such as dill, mustard, caraway, etc.

INSTRUCTIONS:

Prepare the brine by completely dissolving salt in 4 cups of water.

Wash radishes well and remove tops and tails. Cut small radishes into quarters and larger ones into sixths.

Place spices or seasonings in the bottom of a quart jar. Pack radishes on top of seasonings and cover with brine, leaving about 1 inch of headspace.

If necessary, weigh radishes down under the brine to keep them submerged.

Cover the jar with a tight lid, airlock lid, or coffee filter secured with a rubber band.

Culture at room temperature (60-70°F is preferred) until desired flavor and texture are achieved. If using a tight lid, burp daily to release excess pressure.

Once radishes are finished culturing, put a tight lid on the jar and move to cold storage.

LACTO-FERMENTED PEARL ONIONS

INGREDIENTS:

1½ tsp. sea salt

1 q uart unchlorinated water

2 Tbsp. mustard seeds

2 Tbsp. black peppercorns

2 lbs. pearl onions

2 bay leaves

2 sprigs tarragon

1-2 black currant or grape leaves

INSTRUCTIONS:

Make brine by dissolving sea salt in water.

Mix the mustard seeds with the peppercorns in a little bowl and set it aside.

Peel the pearl onions carefully and rinse thoroughly in cold water.

Sprinkle a bit of the mustard/peppercorn mixture into the bottom of a clean quart jar. Add a layer of onions. Fill the jar by layering onions and sprinkled-in layers of the spices.

Once the jar is full, slide the tarragon and bay leaves into the jar, against the sides.

Pour the chilled brine over the onions and spices, filling the jar to 1 inch below the rim. Cover the onions with the grape or currant leaves; add a fermentation weight on top of the leaves to keep the onions submerged in the brine.

Seal the jar tightly with a lid or airlock and ferment away from drafts and direct sunlight for about 2 to 3 days at room temperature, or until the brine turns cloudy.

When the brine begins to get cloudy, move the jar to cold storage (cellar or refrigerator).

LACTO-FERMENTED CORN AND ONION RELISH

INGREDIENTS:

1 medium tomato

1 small onion

2 cloves fresh garlic

3-4 sprigs fresh cilantro

3 cups fresh, washed corn kernels

1 red bell pepper

1/4 tsp. hot pepper flakes

1 Tbsp. sea salt

Filtered room-temperature water

INSTRUCTIONS:

Blanch tomatoes to remove peels, then cut into cubes. Finely dice onion, garlic, and cilantro.

Mix together in a medium bowl. Add corn, pepper, and pepper flakes; sprinkle with salt and mix well. Use a wooden spoon or Cabbage Crusher to lightly press the ingredients to release the juices.

Pour all the ingredients into a q uart jar, pressing slightly to pack and fill the jar to 1 inch below the rim. Pour in water to cover the vegetables completely. If necessary, weigh them down under the brine to keep them submerged.

Cover the jar with a tight lid, airlock lid, or coffee filter secured with a rubber band

Culture at room temperature (60-70°F is preferred) until desired flavor is achieved. If using a tight lid, burp daily to release excess pressure.

Once the relish is finished, put a tight lid on the jar and move to cold storage.

LACTO-FERMENTED WATERMELON RIND PICKLES

INGREDIENTS:

Rind from one or more watermelons

Sea salt

Filtered water

Spices as desired

INSTRUCTIONS:

Scrape the pink flesh from the watermelon rind. Peel the outer green skin from the watermelon rind. Cut the watermelon rind into 1-inch squares.

Prepare light brine by combining 1-3 Tbsp. of salt and 1 quart of filtered water.

Place watermelon rind sq uares and any spices you desire into a fermentation vessel. Fill up the remaining space in the jar with the salt solution. Use a wooden or plastic utensil to release any air bubbles trapped along the sides of the jar.

If necessary, weigh the rind pieces down under the brine.

Cover each jar with a tight lid, airlock lid, or coffee filter secured with a rubber band.

Culture at room temperature (60-70°F is preferred) until desired flavor and texture are achieved. If using a tight lid, burp daily to release excess pressure.

Once the culture is finished, put a tight lid on the jar and move to cold storage. The flavor will continue to develop.

LACTO-FERMENTED CARROT AND PARSNIP PICKLES

INGREDIENTS:

1 pound parsnips

1 pound carrots

1 tsp. fresh grated ginger

1/4 tsp. red pepper flakes

2 Tbsp. sea salt

4 cups water

INSTRUCTIONS:

Wash parsnips and carrots well. Remove tops and cut lengthwise into small sticks. Cutting the sticks tall enough to fill jar 1 1/2 inches below the rim is helpful for even packing.

Place grated ginger and red pepper flakes in the bottom of a quart jar. Place parsnip and carrot sticks atop ginger and red pepper flakes, trying to line them up and pack them in as evenly as possible. Leave 1 inch of headspace at the top of the jar.

Make a brine of 4 cups water to 2 Tbsp. sea salt. Stir to dissolve salt and pour over vegetables, leaving 1 inch of headspace.

Place the lid on the jar or add the airlock, if using. Ferment at room temperature 5-10 days. If not using an airlock, burp the jars daily to release the fermentation gases.

Once the initial fermentation period is over, and the carrots and parsnips are as tangy as desired, move jar to cold storage.

LACTO-FERMENTED RAW SWEET POTATOES

INGREDIENTS:

5 pounds sweet potatoes, with any surface dirt rinsed off, sliced very thinly

1 1/2-inch piece of fresh ginger, peeled and grated

1 large onion, diced

1 tsp. cayenne powder

3-4 Tbsp. sea salt

INSTRUCTIONS:

In a large bowl combine sweet potato slices with ginger, onion, and cayenne powder. Sprinkle with salt to taste.

Pound the sweet potatoes a bit with a Cabbage Crusher or potato masher to encourage the release of the juices and to help the brine develop faster.

Once the brine begins to form, transfer to a fermentation vessel and weigh down with weights. Push down with a clean hand, if necessary, until the brine goes above the vegetables.

Cover and ferment 5-10 days. It is important to keep this ferment in a cool place (under 65°F) as a quick fermentation could result in a large amount of alcohol being produced.

If you are not using an airlock, be sure to burp the jars regularly to release pressure.

Once the potatoes are pleasantly fermented, move them to cold storage. If the fermenting environment has become warmer, move the potatoes to cold storage after 2-3 days, and leave them to ferment for another 1-2 weeks.

CHAPTER SIX

FRUITS PICKLES

GINGER HONEY PICKLED PEACHES

Serves: 4 Prep Time: 15 Minutes Cooking Time: 10 Minutes
Print Recipe

INGREDIENTS

2-3 TJ's Peaches

1 cup TJ's Apple Juice or TJ's Dixie Peach Juice

1 cup TJ's Apple Cider Vinegar

1/4 cup TJ's Mesquite Honey

2 Tbsp peeled & chopped TJ's Ginger

1/2 tsp TJ's Ground Cinnamon

DIRECTIONS

To peel the peaches, blanch in boiling water for about 2 minutes then immediately transfer with a slotted spoon to a bowl of ice water. Once peaches have cooled a minute or two, gently slide the skins off with your fingertips. Cut peaches in half, remove pits then cut into quarters. To make the pickling brine, combine fruit juice, vinegar, honey, ginger and cinnamon in a medium sized nonreactive pot (any pot EXCEPT that made of aluminum, cast iron or copper). Bring to a boil, reduce heat and simmer for 3-5 minutes. To pickle the peaches, add peach segments and cook just until tender, about 3-5 minutes. Carefully remove peaches with a slotted spoon and transfer to a glass jar with a reseal able lid. Let pickling mixture cool slightly and then pour over peaches. Seal with lid and store in the refrigerator. Ready to eat immediately, but will develop more flavor overnight. Each batch should keep for an additional week or two in the refrigerator. If any off flavors or smells develop, or if you notice fermentation, please discard. Pairing & Serving Suggestions: Perfect served alongside roasted chicken or ham, warmed and spooned over vanilla ice cream, or even pureed and mixed into a cocktail (try it with sparkling grape juice, prosecco or bourbon)...

QUICK PICKLED STRAWBERRIES

Prep time: 10 hours Cook time: 10 mins Total time: 10 hours 10 mins

Serves: 12

Ingredients

1 lb. ripe, but firm fresh strawberries

½ cup plus 2 Tbsp. white balsamic vinegar (can use red wine vinegar or apple cider vinegar)

½ cup plus 2 Tbsp. granulated sugar or evaporated cane juice

½ cup plus 2 Tbsp. water

1 sprig fresh rosemary

¼ vanilla bean (I used one I had in a jar of sugar)

Instructions

Rinse strawberries well and trim off green leaves and any bruised spots. Quarter the largest berries, and halve the smaller ones. Place into a sterilized quart canning jar with the rosemary sprig and vanilla bean.

In a small pan combine the white balsamic vinegar, sugar, and water. Bring to a boil and pour over the strawberries, leaving a little room at the top. Replace the can lid and ring. Tighten. Let cool to room temperature and chill overnight before using.

Keep refrigerated. Best eaten within two weeks.

QUICK PICKLED BLUEBERRIES, GOAT CHEESE, HONEY, PLUOT, SAGE, PISTACHIO TARTINEs

Ingredients

2 cups blueberries

1 cup red wine vinegar (I wanted the sour taste to be prominent, so I used only vinegar, but feel free to substitute water for part of the vinegar. I probably wouldn't go over 1/2 cup of water)

3 tablespoons wild dandelion honey

1 cinnamon stick

2 inch orange peel

1/2 teaspoon fennel seeds

1/4 teaspoon whole cloves

1/4 teaspoon whole tellicherry peppercorns

1/2 teaspoon juniper berries

1 teaspoon kosher salt

4 ounces goat cheese

3 ounces cold cream cheese

chopped salted pistachios

wild dandelion honey

pluot, sliced

torn sage leaves

goat cheese spread

pickled blueberries

slices of good q uality bread

Instructions

In a small pot, bring the vinegar (and water, if using), honey, cinnamon, orange peel, fennel, cloves, peppercorns, juniper berries, and salt to boil. Place the blueberries in a mason jar, then pour the vinegar mixture over the berries. Refrigerate overnight.

In mixer, beat goat cheese with the cream cheese.

To assemble the tartines: Spread goat cheese mixture on bread. Brush on a bit of honey. Add pluot slices, sage leaves, pickled blueberries, and chopped pistachios.

PICKLED BLACKBERRIES

INGREDIENTS

300g/11 oz blackberries

100ml/3 1/2 fl oz white wine vinegar

200g/7 oz sugar

1 rose geranium leaf (optional)

DIRECTONS

Pick over the blackberries and rinse under cold water and then pat dry.

Heat the blackberries along with the sugar and vinegar in a heavy based pan over a gentle heat until the sugar has completely dissolved.

Simmer the fruit for 5 minutes then carefully remove with a slotted spoon and pack into a sterilized jar.

Raise the temperature and boil the vinegar until it becomes thick and syrup like.

Add the geranium leaf to the jar and pour over the hot vinegar.

Pop on a lid and store in a cool dark place for 1 month before using.

Once opened store in the fridge for up to 2 weeks.

PICKLED PLUMS

Ingredients:

2-1/2 pounds assorted plums (about 10)

2 medium red onions

2 cups water

2 cups red-wine vinegar

2-1/4 cups sugar

3 cinnamon sticks

1-1/2 teaspoons whole allspice

1/2 teaspoon whole cloves

1/2 teaspoon salt

Directions:

1) Pit plums and cut into 1/2-inch wedges. Cut onions into 3/4-inch pieces and transfer with plums to a 10-cup (2 1/2-quart) heatproof glass jar with a lid.

2) Place vinegar, water, sugar, cinnamon sticks, allspice, cloves and salt in a large saucepan. Bring to a boil, stirring until sugar is dissolved. Immediately pour over plums and onions.

3) Cool mixture, uncovered. Refrigerate, covered, for at least 6 hours. Pickled plums can be kept, refrigerated, for 1 week. Yield: 12 servings.

PICKLED WATERMELON RIND

Ingredients:

rind of 1/2 large watermelon

For the brine:

1 cups hot water

1/2cup rice wine vinegar

6 tbsp granulated sugar

2 and 1/4 tsp salt

1 tsp mustard seeds

1 star anise, optional

Method:

1. After removing the flesh of the water melon, use a Swiss peeler to remove the dark green skin of the watermelon wedges.

2. Cut the watermelon rind into 1 cm by 1 cm cubes. It is okay to have a little of the red flesh on.

3. Place the cubed watermelon rind into a pot and fill it with tap water. Add in two big pinches of salt and bring the water to a boil.

4. Allow the water to boil for about 3 – 5 minutes (depending how soft you like it) before turning of the heat and draining the watermelon rind in a colander.

5. Prepare the brine by mixing all the ingredients in a large mixing bowl and stir to dissolve the sugar and salt before adding the rind to it.

6. Once it is done, store the rind and the brine liq uid (it should cover the top of the rind) insterilized glass jars (mason jars work well) in the refrigerator. You can begin eating them in a few hours but they are best served after standing overnight in the fridge.

*To sterilize the glass jar, wash the jar and lid with hot water and soap. Rinse well and place the jar in a preheated oven at 160 degrees Celsius for 10 minutes or until dry.

*The pickled watermelon rind will keep for a week in the fridge.

SPICY PICKLED GRAPES

Makes 1 pound (about 2 cups)

1 1/2 cups apple cider vinegar

1 cup brown sugar

1 cup of water

6 fresh ginger slices, about 1/4-inch thick

3 star anise

1/2 teaspoon sichuan peppercorns

2 tablespoons coriander

2 cinnamon sticks

1 bay leaf

1 pound red grapes, picked, rinsed clean and drained

METHOD

In a non-reactive pan, combine everything but the grapes and bring to a simmer to dissolve the sugar.

 Place the grapes in a bowl that can take heat and pour the brine over. Let steep until cool. Store in glass jars in the refrigerator up to one month.

SPICY PICKLED PINEAPPLE

Prep Time20 MIN

Cook Time 20 MINS

INGREDIENTS

1/2 pineapple cut into half circles

1 1/2 cup Nakano citrus seasoned rice vinegar

1 tablespoon sugar

1 large jalapeno, sliced into circles

1/2 tablespoon kosher salt juice of 2 limes

1/4 cup roughly chopped cilantro

INSTRUCTIONS

Place the vinegar, sugar, jalapeno, salt and lime juice in a small sauce pot. Bring to a simmer stir until sugar dissolves, remove from heat and let cool to room temperature.

Place the pineapple and cilantro into a large jar.

Pour the vinegar mixture over the pineapple; it should just cover the top slice.

Seal and refrigerate at least 1 day before eating.

Store in the refrigerator for up to 2 weeks. Pineapple will become tangier with time.

DETOXIFYING AMALAKI/AMLA PICKLE (INDIAN GOOSEBERRY)

PREP TIME 5 mins

COOK TIME 20 mins

TOTAL TIME 25 mins

INGREDIENTS

Fresh Raw Amla Fruits (one bowl - 20 pieces)

1 Tablespoon coconut oil or olive oil (or any vegetable oil)

½ teaspoon salt

½ teaspoon cumin seeds

½ teaspoon Turmeric powder

INSTRUCTIONS

Wash Raw Amla Fruits nicely

In a Pan or Skillet, add 1 tablespoon of oil

on a low heat, add raw Amla Fruits

Add in the salt, cumin seeds, Turmeric Powder to the Pan

Stir to mix all the spices well with the Amla

Cover with the lid and cook on low heat for (15-20 min). Check occasionally to ensure no sticking in the pan.

It is cooked when Amla fruit is tender and easy to slice in pieces.

Once cooled, store in a glass Jar and refrigerate.

LEMON PICKLE

Ingredients

2 lemons

1 small fresh red chilli

2 tablespoons olive oil

1 tablespoon yellow mustard seeds

1 teaspoon cumin seeds

1 small handful curry leaves

3 tablespoons caster sugar

Method

Wash and finely chop the lemons, discarding the pips, then deseed and finely slice the chilli.

Heat the oil in a small pan over a low heat and add the mustard and cumin seeds. When they start to pop, throw in the curry leaves. Fry for a minute or so, until they're nice and crisp.

Add the lemons, sugar, chilli and a pinch of sea salt. Turn up to a medium heat and cook for around 10 minutes, or until thick, sticky and the lemons have softened.

Leave to cool, then store in a sterilized jar in the fridge, where it will keep for up to a week. Delicious served with poppadoms, plain yoghurt and a red onion and tomato salad.

PICKLED PLUMS AND ONIONS RECIPE

Ingredients

2 cups plums

2 cups Creole onions

1-½ cups white balsamic vinegar

1/3 cup agave nectar

1 tablespoon salt

2 cloves garlic, cut in thirds

1 fresh bay leaf, torn in half

1 teaspoon pink, green and black peppercorn medley

½ teaspoon mustard seeds

½ teaspoon juniper berries

4 cloves

2 green cardamom pods

Directions

The day before...

Trim both ends of the onions. Remove the stalks and reserve them for another dish (they are very flavorful). Peel the onions.

Pack the onions in a jar. Sprinkle with salt and cover with water, Allow to cure for a day (up to 18 hours).

The next day.

Canning the jar:

Drain the liquid, rinse and drain one more time.

In a saucepan, combine the vinegar and agave nectar. Bring to a boil, then immediately reduce the heat to a gentle simmer for 10 minutes. Allow the mixture to cool.

While the brine is simmering, fill a deep saucepan and bring to just under a boil. Place a 1-liter jar, lid, heat-proof funnel and tongs in the pot and boil for 10 minutes. Be sure to read the instructions that come with the jar. They'll give you exact time and techniq ues.

Remove the jar from the water.

Place the onions in the jar.

Wash the plums. Cut the fruit in half and use your fingers to remove the pits.

In a mortar and pestle, crush the pods of cardamoms and extract the black seeds.

Add the bay leaf, garlic, peppercorns, mustard seeds, cloves, cardamom seeds and juniper berries to the jar. Complete and fill the jar with the halved plums. Tightly pack them. Fill the jar with the brine to cover the food, leaving about ¼-inch of head space or whatever your canning directions say.

Carefully place the lid on the jar, using a magnet (see tips). Tighten the collar around the jar. Bring your large pot of water to a boil and place the sealed jar in it for 10 minutes.

Remove the jar from the water. If the top of the lid still pops, the vacuum didn't form and you'll need to consume the pickles in the next several weeks, storing it in the refrigerator. Otherwise you can safely store it in your pantry for up to a year.

For optimal flavor, allow about 6 weeks before opening the jar.

PICKLED PEARS

INGREDIENTS

For each 500 ml jar: (7 in total need to be sterilized)

3 juniper berries

2 peppercorns

2 cloves

1x3 inch slice of orange peel

4 q t basket of sugar pears

Brine:

8 cups vinegar (I used a light red wine one)

4 cups sugar

INSTRUCTIONS

Prepare the jars with spices and peel. Fill each with peeled pears and top with hot brine mixture. Top and process in a water bath for 14 minutes. Let sit at least two weeks before enjoying.

PICKLED APPLE SLICES

Yield: 6 pints

Ingredients

10-14 apples (peeled, cored, sliced)

5 cups white sugar

3/4 cup apple cider vinegar

3 cups water

juice of 1 lemon

2 Tbsp whole cloves

6 cinnamon sticks

1 inch piece of ginger (chopped)

Instructions

In a large-sized, non-ionized pot combine all ingredients but apples. Bring to a boil and cook for 3 minutes.

Add 2 cored, sliced, peeled apples to each hot, clean largemouth pint jar.

Ladle brine ingredients over apples leaving approx.1/4 inch headspace.

Wipe rims, apply lids and rings (finger tight) and then process jars in hot water bath for 12 minutes. Remove canner from heat and let jars remain in hot water bath for 5 minutes (this will help prevent syphoning).

Remove jars from canner and let cool on a folded towel for 12-24 hours.

Store jars in a cool, dry place for at least a week before serving. Shelf life up to 1 year.

PICKLED PEACHES

INGREDIENTS

6x500 ml jars (sterilized)

In each jar:

1 clove

2 inch x 1 inch lemon peel

½ inch candied ginger

For the brine:

4 cups sugar

4 cups vinegar (I used light red wine vinegar)

1 cup honey

4 quart basket of peaches

INSTRUCTIONS

Bring brine ingredients to a boil.

Prepare jars with lemon peel, ginger, cloves and enough sliced peaches to fill. I sliced the peaches (skin on) roughly 1½ inches thick.

Fill jars with the brine mix, top and process in a water bath for 14 minutes. Let sit for at least a week before enjoying.

SWEET PICKLED CHERRIES

1 3/4 cups apple cider vinegar

1 3/4 cups sugar

3/4 cup water

3 cinnamon sticks

2 pounds sweet cherries with stems and pits intact

DIRECTION

Prepare your jars and lids. Jars should be kept warm in the canner.

Combine vinegar, sugar, and water in a medium saucepan. Bring to a boil and simmer until sugar is dissolved.

Remove hot jars from canner. Pack each jar with cherries, and add one cinnamon stick to each jar. Pour hot syrup over cherries leaving 1/2 inch headspace. Wipe jar rims and place lids and rings on each. Process 15 minutes in a boiling water bath. Remove jars from canner and cool.

PICKLED CHERRIES WITH FIVE SPICES

Prep time: 20 mins

Cook time: 30 mins

Total time: 50 mins

Serves: 6 to 8 cups

Ingredients

2 lbs fresh cherries (I used dark cherries) stems and pits intact

3 cups red wine vinegar

1 cup sugar

1 1/2 Tablespoons salt

1 teaspoon Szechuan peppercorns

3 cinnamon sticks

1/2 teaspoon all spice

3 pieces of star anise

2 teaspoons whole cloves

Instructions

With a small fork or a toothpick, puncture each cherry 5-6 times to allow the pickling juice to penetrate the fruit. Place the cherries into a glass jar.

In a medium pot, mix together the all the spices and the salt and bring to a boil.

Reduce the heat and let the mixture simmer for 15-20 minutes, or until the liquid is reduced to 1/3 of its original amount.

Remove the pot from heat and let the pickling liq uid cool down for 10 minutes.

Pour the liquid over the cherries in the jar.

If the cherries are not fully submerged, that's okay. In a few hours, they will release more juice into the pickling liq uid.

Let the cherries cool down completely before closing the lid.

Keep the pickled cherries in the sealed jars in the refrigerator.

The pickled cherries, refrigerated, will keep up to one month. The longer they keep, the more wrinkly and the more pale they will become.

BALSAMIC PICKLED FRUIT

INGREDIENTS

2 cups ripe berries or cherries

1 cup balsamic vinegar

1/2 cup water

1 cinnamon stick

4 allspice berries

6 pink peppercorns

2 cloves

INSTRUCTIONS

Wash and sterilize jars and lids.

Wash fruit, you can remove stems and pits, but you don't have to - personal preference.

Put fruit into jars leaving ¼ inch space at the top.

Over medium heat combine water, balsamic vinegar, cinnamon, allspice, peppercorns and cloves.

Let simmer 8-10 min then remove cinnamon stick, (I left the rest of the spices in).

Pour into jars over the packed fruit, again leaving ¼ inch at the top.

I immersed the jars in a boiling water bath for 15 min, removed and let cool.

Allow to sit 24-48 hours before serving.

PICKLED RAINIER CHERRIES

PREP TIME 10 mins

COOK TIME 5 mins

TOTAL TIME 15 mins

INGREDIENTS

1 pound (about 50) Rainier cherries, stems trimmed to ½ inch, pitting optional

2 cups white wine vinegar

1½ cups sugar (or less)

Pinch kosher salt

1 small bunch tarragon

2 tablespoons pink peppercorns, divided (I used rainbow peppercorns)

INSTRUCTIONS

In a medium saucepan, bring vinegar, sugar, salt, a few springs of tarragon and 1 tablespoon of peppercorns to a boil.

Reduce the heat, simmer until the sugar and salt dissolve and set aside to cool.

Meanwhile, load the cherries into a glass jar(s) with 10-12 peppercorns and a few sprigs of tarragon. Pour the cooled brine over the cherries to cover them, place the lid on and refrigerate.

After a few days (I waited a week), your cherries are ready!! (!!!) Yay. You can keep them in the fridge for up to a year, if you don't gobble them before then.

PICKLED BLACKBERRIES

PREP TIME 15mins

COOK TIME 10mins

TOTAL TIME 25mins

INGREDIENTS

8 black peppercorns

3 allspice berries

2 juniper berries

½-inch piece of fresh ginger, thinly sliced

1 small fresh bay leaf

1 sprig fresh thyme

1 shallot, quartered lengthwise

6 tbsps. sugar

3 tbsps. kosher salt

2 cups red wine vinegar

2 cups water

18 oz. fresh blackberries (about 4 cups), washed and shaken of excess water

INSTRUCTIONS

Roughly crush the peppercorns, allspice, and juniper berries together with a mortar and pestle (or however you like to crush hard round spices). Place the crushed spices, ginger, bay leaf, sprig of thyme, shallot, sugar, kosher salt, red wine vinegar, and water in a medium saucepan. Bring the brine to a boil, stirring to dissolve the salt and sugar.

Remove the saucepan from the heat and strain the liquid. Let the liquid cool completely or you'll cook your berries. Discard the spices and aromatics.

Place the berries in a clean canning jars. Pour the cooled pickling liq uid over the berries. Cover the jar tightly and refrigerate for at least a week before serving, but 2 or more weeks is preferred. Keeps for up to 3 months refrigerated. Makes 4 cups of pickled blackberries.

SWEET DRIED FRUIT PICKLE

INGREDIENTS

250g mixed dried fruit

1/2cup brown vinegar

1 1/2 teaspoons mustard powder

1 1/2 teaspoons chili powder

¼ cup sunflower oil

1 teaspoon turmeric

1 teaspoon salt

1 teaspoon crushed fresh garlic

3 tablespoons sugar

1 teaspoon whole cloves

4 cinnamon sticks

1 1/2 teaspoons whole black peppercorns

3 tablespoons golden syrup

COOKING INSTRUCTIONS

Pour boiling water over the fruits and drain.

Slice each piece of fruit into strips.

Place in a large bowl. Pour vinegar into a cup and stir in mustard and chili powder.

Pour over the fruit in the bowl.

Add remaining ingredients.

Mix well and store in a clean jar.

CHAPTER SEVEN

KIMCHI RECIPES

GREEN ONION POLLOCK KIMCHI

Ingredients

1-1/2 lb. spring green onion

1/4 lb. dried shredded pollock

1 cup anchovy stock

1 tablespoon sweet rice flour

1/2 cup Korean chili flakes

1/2 sweet apple, peeled, seeded, diced

1-inch ginger, peeled, diced

2 teaspoons sugar

4 tablespoons Korean anchovy sauce

2 tablespoons black sesame seeds, optional

Instructions

Slice green onion to 2" pieces and put them in a large mixing bowl. Sprinkle 1 table spoon of anchovy sauce and toss. Let it sit for 10 minutes.

Meanwhile, water and sweet rice flour in a small pot and place the pot over medium high heat. Cook the mixture until thickens, about, 2-3 minutes, as whisking continuously. Remove from the heat and set aside to cook.

In a blender, puree together apple, ginger, and the rest of fish sauce until smooth.

Combine the rice glue, apple ginger puree with Korean chili flakes in a bowl and add sugar; mix well to make the seasoning paste.

Add the seasoning paste to the green onion in a large bowl, add in the dried pollock, and black sesame seeds; toss to incorporate all.

Line an airtight glass container with a large plastic bag. Put the kimchi inside the plastic bag and tie to seal. Close the lid and let it sit in the room temperature for 2 days, then store in the fridge for another 3-4 days. Serve the kimchi with any korean meal.

Notes

To make anchovy stock, simmer 5-6 large dried anchovies in 2 cups of water for 10 minutes. Discard the anchovies and reserve the stock.

POPULAR KOREAN CABBAGE KIMCHI

Ingredients

2 heads nappa cabbage, about 5 lb. each

1 cup Korean sea salt plus extra 1/2 cup

15 cups water

1/2 apple, cored and peeled

1/2 onion, diced

1 head garlic, peeled

1-inch ginger, peeled

1/2 medium Korea radish, sliced into very thin matchsticks

1 bunch green onion, sliced

1-1/2 cup Korean chili flakes

1/2 cup Korean fish sauce

1/2 cup Korean shrimp sauce

For fruit stock

10 cups water

2 small sweet apples, sliced

1 onion, cut into wedge

1 Asian leek, diced

2 tablespoons gugija, Chinese dried matrimony vine berries

5 piece dried sea kelp

For rice glue

1 cup fruit stock

1 tablespoon sweet rice flour

Instructions

Cut the cabbage in half and give 2-inch slit on the stem part of each half. Rinse the cabbage.

Using 1/2 cup of salt, sprinkle into white stem parts of cabbage toward the stem. Place the cabbage in a large container or in the sink. Dissolve 1 cup of salt with 15 cups of water and pour over the cabbage. Press the cabbage to let the salt solution to sip through. Place a heavy object such as bricks or heavy cast iron skillet on top of cabbage. Let them soak for 8-12 hours turning them to the other side during the soaking time. When the stem part of cabbage is bending without breaking, they are ready. Separate the split cabbage half completely.

Rinse the cabbage 2-3 times in the water and place them in a large colander to drain. Press gently to remove excess water.

To make the fruit stock; combine all the ingredients and bring them to boil. Turn the heat to low, and simmer for 50 minutes. Reserve the stock and discard the rest.

To make the rice glue; whisk together 1 cup of the fruit stock and 1 tablespoon of sweet rice flour. Cook over medium heat until it gets bubbly and thicken whisking constantly, about 2-3 minutes. Remove from the heat and let it cool.

To make kimchi seasoning paste; put apple slices, onion, garlic, ginger with fish sauce in a blender and process until smooth. You can add a few tablespoons of fruit stock to help the blender blade to run better. Transfer the puree into a large mixing bowl and add radish, green onion, shrimp sauce, and the rice glue. Mix well with a wooden spoon and set aside for 10 minutes.

To assemble; Line your container with a clean plastic bag and set aside.

Place each cabbage onto a shallow mixing bowl; spread a little amount of seasoning paste onto the outer leaf of the cabbage first, then moving onto the next layer one leaf at a time. Spread just enough to cover entire leaf. When all the leaves are covered, gather up the leafy part of the cabbage toward the stem and wrap the whole thing with the most outer large leaf to make a bundle to secure everything inside.

Place the kimchi in side of the plastic bag and stack them tightly together. When finished, tie the bag tightly to keep the air out. Cover with a lid and let the whole thing sit on the room temperature for 1-2 days depends on the weather. Store the kimchi in the fridge after that. Your kimchi should be ready to serve in next 3-5 days. This kimchi can last months stored in the fridge and it will continue to ferment developing more sour flavor as time goes.

TURNIP GREEN KIMCHI

Ingredients

1.5 lb turnip greens, rinsed

1/4 cup Korean coarse sea salt

1-1/2 cup water

5-6 large dried anchovies

1 piece dried sea kelp

2 dried shiitake mushrooms

1 tablespoon sweet rice flour

1/4 lb fresh red chilies, diced

1/2 onion, diced

3-4 cloves garlic

1" piece ginger

1/4 cup Korean chili flakes

3 tablespoons anchovy sauce

1 tablespoon shrimp sauce

Instructions

In a large shallow bowl, lay a few turnip greens on the bottom. Sprinkle a little bit, about 1/2 tablespoonful, of sea salt on top. Repeat the layers and sprinkle with salt until all the turnip greens covered with salt. You might need more salt depends on the volume.

Let them sit on the counter for 1 hour, turn upside down half way. They will reduce in volume by half. Rinse the turnip green with water a couple of times. Drain and set aside.

Meanwhile, make a stock. Combine 1-1/2 cups of water dried anchovies, sea kelp, and the dried mushrooms in a small pot. Bring to a gentle boil, and then simmer for 5 minutes over low heat. Remove the pot from heat and let it cool for 5 minutes. Reserve 1 cup + 2 tablespoons of stock and discard the rest.

To make rice glue, in a small pot whisk together 1 cup of reserved stock and sweet rice flour. Bring to med-high heat and let them bubble whisking continuously until it gets thicken. Remove from heat and set aside to cool.

In a blender, puree onion, red chili, garlic, ginger, anchovy sauce, shrimp sauce until semi-smooth. Pour the mixture in a large mixing bowl. Add the Korean red chili flakes, the reserved rice glue; mix well.

Add the turnip greens and toss gently with your hand to incorporate with the seasoning.

Transfer the turnip green kimchi into an airtight container and let it sit in the room temperature for 2 days, then store in the fridge afterward. Your kimchi should be ready to eat 2-3 days.

Notes

Turnip green kimchi can last in the fridge about 2 months. They are still edible after the 2 months but it will be very potent and sour.

GARLIC CHIVES KIMCHI

Ingredients

10 oz. garlic chives, cleaned and cut in 2-3 lengthwise

1 cup water

4-5 large dried anchovies

1/2 small onion, diced

2 garlic cloves

1/2-inch ginger, diced

1/3 cup Korean chili flakes

1 tablespoon salted shrimps

2-3 tablespoon anchovy sauce or other fish sauce

2 teaspoon sugar

Instructions

In a small pot, add water and dried anchovies, bring to gentle boil and simmer for 5-7 minutes. Reserve 1/2 cup of stock and discard the rest.

Combine onion, garlic, ginger and the anchovy stock in a blender and process until smooth.

In a large mixing bowl, combine the puree above, chili flakes, salted shrimps, 2 tablespoons anchovy sauce (or fish sauce), and sugar. Mix well.

Add the chives and toss well to coat. Taste the kimchi and adjust the seasoning according to your taste.

Transfer the chive kimchi into an airtight container and let it ferment in a room temperature for 1-2 days, then store in the fridge for 2 more days before you serve. Serve with rice and other Korean dishes.

GREEN CABBAGE KIMCHI

Ingredients

1 large head (about 3.5 lb.) green cabbage

4 tablespoons coarse sea salt

3 cloves garlic

1/2-inch piece ginger

3 tablespoons anchovy sauce

2 tablespoons cooked white rice (short grain preferred) *

6 tablespoons water

7 tablespoons Korean chili flakes

1 tablespoon shrimp sauce

1 tablespoon sugar

3 green onion, chopped

1/2 to 1 cup water

Instructions

Cut and dice the cabbage into 1-1/2 inch pieces. Try to separate the cabbage layers. Rinse them well and place them in a large mixing bowl. Sprinkle sea salt over and toss well. Let them sit for 2 hour turning once or twice during the time.

Rinse the cabbage once and drain well. Set aside.

In a blender, combine garlic, ginger, anchovy sauce, cooked rice, and the 6 tablespoons of water. Puree them until very smooth.

In a large mixing bowl, combine Korean chili flakes, shrimp sauce, sugar, and the rice puree. Mix well. Add the cabbage and the green onion. Toss well to incorporate the seasoning to the cabbage.

Transfer the kimchi into an airtight container. Pour 1/2 to 1 cup of water into a mixing bowl and swirl around the collect the seasoning paste reside inside the bowl. Pour it back to the kimchi.

Cover the kimchi with the lid and let it sit on a counter for 1 day and then, store in the refrigerator for 3-4 more days for better fermentation.

Notes

* Instead of cooked rice you can make the rice glue with sweet rice flour. Mix 1 cup of water with 1 tablespoon of sweet rice flour. Bring to boil and cook until thickened. Use about 1/3 cup for this recipe and freeze the rest for another use.

GREEN ONION KIMCHE

Prep Time25 min Cook Time5 min Total Time30 min

Ingredients

3 bundles (about 3/4 lbs) thin green onions, trimmed

4 tablespoon anchovy sauce

1 tablespoon sweet rice flour

2/3 cup water

6 tablespoon Korean chili flakes

1 teaspoon sugar

2 cloves garlic, finely minced

1 teaspoon freshly grated ginger

1 tablespoon Korean corn syrup, optional

Toasted sesame seeds for garnish

Instructions

Place green onions on a baking sheet, sprinkle 2 tablespoon of anchovy sauce over white part of green onions. Toss to coat and set aside.

In a small sauce pan, mix sweet rice flour with water. Cook the mixture until it thickens whisking constantly over medium heat. Set aside to cool down a little.

In a small mixing bowl, mix chili flakes, sugar, the remaining anchovy sauce, garlic, ginger, and corn syrup if using.

Spread the chili paste onto green onion all over. Take 3-4 green onions and fold, wrap around with green parts to secure into bundles. Put the bundles into an airtight container and let it ferment in a room temperature for 1- 2 days, then store in the refrigerator for 3-4 days before you eat.

You can serve the kimchi as a whole piece or cut into 2 -inch slices. Serve as a side dish with rice and main dish.

CUBED RADISH KIMCHI

Ingredients

2 medium size Korean radish

1/4 cup Korean coarse sea salt

2 tablespoon sugar

5 tablespoon Korean chili flakes

1/2 large onion, diced

3 cloves garlic

1″ piece ginger, chopped

2 tablespoon salted shrimps

5 tablespoon milk

1-2 tablespoon anchovy sauce

2 tablespoon Korean corn syrup or 1 tablespoon sugar

2 green onion diced Coupons

Instructions

Clean the radish with a kitchen brush and rise well. Slice it into 3/4-1 inch disks, and then slice into cubes.

Place the radish cubes in a large mixing bowl or in a kitchen sink (with the drainage closed), sprinkle salt and 2 tablespoon sugar, and toss well. Let them sit for 45-60 minutes tossing once to soak evenly. Rinse the radish once and drain well.

Put the radish in a large mixing bowl and sprinkle 1 tablespoon of Korean chili flakes and toss. Set aside.

In a blender, combine onion, garlic, ginger, salted shrimps, and milk. Process until smooth. Transfer to a mixing bowl and add 4 tablespoon Korean chili flakes, anchovy sauce, and corn syrup (or sugar). Mix well and let it sit for 5 minutes.

Combine the radish cubes and green onion, pour the chili filling, and toss all together until every radish cubes are well coated with the filling. Taste and adjust seasoning with more anchovy sauce and sugar according to your taste.

Transfer the radish kimchi into an airtight container and let it sit in the room temperature for 1-2 days, then store in the refrigerator for 7 days for a good fermentation before you serve. Enjoy!

BACHELOR KIMCHI

Ingredients

3-1/4 lb young radish bunches

1/2 cup coarse sea salt

one handful dried pollock or 5-6 dried large anchovies

2 tablespoon sweet rice flour

2 cups water

1/4 onion, diced

1/4 apple, peeled and diced

4 cloves garlic

1/2" piece ginger

3 tablespoon anchovy sauce

1 tablespoon salted shrimps (optional)

2 teaspoon sugar

1/2 cup Korean chili flakes

Directions

Clean the radish by scraping off the dirty surface and cut off the tail. Keep the green leafy stem part is attached to the radish. Cut the white part of radish in half of q uarter if they are too big. Rinse them well.

In a large shallow bowl on in a kitchen sink, place the radishes and sprinkle with sea salt evenly all over. Let them soak for 2 hours, turning once or twice. When the radishes seem wilted and lifeless, rinse in water a couple of times and drain in a colander. Let them sit while you are getting the filling ready.

Meanwhile, in a small pot, combine dried pollock or anchovies with 2 cups of water and bring to boil, simmer for 5 minutes. Strain to reserve 3/4 cup + 2 tablespoon of stock. Discard the fish.

In a small pot, combine 3/4 cup of reserved stock with 2 tablespoon of sweet rice flour. Bring them to med-high heat to boil and thicken, whisking constantly. This is the sweet rice glue (You will only use 1/2 cup of this glue). Let it cool.

In a blender, combine onion, apple, garlic, ginger, salted shrimps (if using), with the reserve 2 tablespoon of fish stock. Puree them until very smooth. Transfer the mixture to a mixing bowl, add 1/2 cup of the reserved sweet rice glue, Korean chili flakes, anchovy sauce, and sugar. Mix well and let it sit for 10 minutes for the chili flakes to soften up.

In a large shallow mixing bowl or a baking pan, place the radishes and smother with the chili mixture. You might need to do this in batches to avoid overflowing. Toss, rub and incorporate the chili mixture to evenly coat the radishes and its leafy stems. Store the radish kimchi in a airtight container and let it sit on the room temperature for 2 days first, then store in the refrigerator for 5 more days. Your bachelor kimchi should be ready to eat. (Toss the kimchi with the kimchi juice on the bottom)

NABAK KIMCHI, THE WATER KIMCHI

Ingredients

15-16 Napa cabbage leaves

3/4 lb Korean radish

1 tablespoon kosher salt

1 tablespoon sweet rice flour

1 cup water

1/2 onion, diced

1/2 large Asian pear, peeled, seeded, and diced

2 cloves garlic

1 teaspoon pureed ginger

1 tablespoon Korean chili flakes

1 liter natural spring water

1 small carrot, thinly sliced (about 1/8" thick)

2 green onion, sliced

1 fresh red chili, thinly sliced, optional

kosher salt or sea salt to taste

1 piece of linen or cotton fabric with slightly loose weave, about 12-inch square in size

A piece of string or yarn, about 12-inch long

Directions

Slice the cabbage leaves into 1" slices discarding the bottom 4-5" of leafy parts. Cut the thick white stem parts in half, if needed. Slice the radish into about 1" square with 1/8" thickness.

Combine the cabbage and the radish in a large bowl and sprinkle salt over and toss. Let it sit for 25-30 minutes. Rinse once and drain. Set aside.

Meanwhile mix sweet rice flour with 1 cup of water in a small sauce pan and bring it to boil, and simmer for 2-3 minutes to thicken. Let it cool.

Combine the onion, garlic, and pear in a blender and process until very smooth. Transfer the puree into a mixing bowl. Add pureed ginger, Korean chili flakes and the rice glue. Stir well.

Line a linen fabric over bowl and pour the chili mixture to the center of the fabric. Gather up the fabric and tie with a string tightly.

In a large container put the cabbage and radish mixture; add the carrot, green onion, and the red chili. Place the chili sash in one corner of the container with a string hanging over, pour the spring water over in the container and toss well. Gently squeeze the sash to release the juice out of the chili mixture.

Season the kimchi broth with salt to your taste. Cover and let it sit in a room temperature for 2 days to ferment first, then keep in the fridge for 3 days before you enjoy.

VEGAN KIMCHI

Ingredients

2 lb Napa cabbage

1 cup Korean coarse sea salt

8 cup water

3/4 lb pumpkin, any kind, sliced into 2-3 chunks

3 dried shiitake mushroom

1 large piece dried sea kelp

2 tablespoon plain mashed potatoes

1/2 large onion, diced

1 persimmon, peeled and cored (or 1/2 sweet apple or Asian pear)

5 cloves garlic

1/2" piece ginger, peeled

3-4 fresh red chilies, diced, optional

4 tablespoon Korean chili flakes

4-5 tablespoon Korean soy sauce for soup

4 green onion cut into 2" slices

1 tablespoon toasted sesame seeds

Directions

Cut off the end part of the cabbage stem and cut the cabbage into 2" slices.

In a mixing bowl dissolve salt in the water. Scatter the cabbage slices in a shallow bowl and pour the salted water over and toss. Let the cabbage soak for 1 hour. Turn the cabbages over and continue to soak for another 1-1.5hr. When done, the stem part of cabbage slice should be bendable without breaking. Rinse the cabbages 3 times and let them drain well. Set aside.

Meanwhile, place pumpkin, mushroom, and sea kelp in a medium sauce pot and pour water just to barely cover them. Bring them to boil and let it simmer for 20 minutes. Cool and discard the vegetables reserving the liq uid stock. Reserve 1/2 cup of stock to use, and freeze the rest of stock for later use.

In a blender put potatoes, onion, persimmon, garlic,ginger and pour in the 1/2 cup of stock. Process them until smooth. Add diced fresh red chilies and pulse to chop them into small pieces.

Pour the onion persimmon puree in to a small mixing bowl, add the Korean chili flakes and 4 tablespoon of Korean soy sauce for soup. Mix well.

In a large shallow bowl (or use jelly roll pan) combine cabbages and green onion, add 2/3 of chili filling and sesame seeds. Wear disposable gloves on your hand and toss everything with your hand to make sure everything gets incorporated with chili filling. Add more filling if needed.

Taste a piece and add more Korean soy sauce for soup to adjust seasoning. It should be slightly saltier that you hoped for.

Transfer your kimchi in a airtight container and let it sit in the room temperature for 1-2 days, then store in the fridge after that. Enjoy your labor of love!

30 MINUTE KIMCHI

Ingredients

1 kg (2 lb) napa cabbage

1/2 cup Korean sea salt

5 cups water

4-5 garlic cloves

1" piece ginger

1 small onion diced

3 tablespoon anchovy sauce

2 teaspoon sugar

5 tablespoon Korean chili flakes

2 tablespoon Koran plum extract for tea, or 2 tablespoon apple juice with 1 teaspoon honey

2 red chilies seeded and thinly sliced, optional

2 tablespoon toasted sesame seeds

Directions

Cut off the stem part of cabbage. Cut each cabbage leaf in half or 3-4 section (depends on the size) vertically. Place the cabbage leaves in a large mixing bowl.

Combine salt and water and bring to a full boil dissolving the salt. Cool down for 5 minutes and pour over cabbages in mixing bowl. Let it sit for 10 minutes, turn the cabbages over to the other side and continue to soak for 5 more minutes. Rinse once and drain thoroughly.

To make kimchi filling, combine garlic, ginger, onion and anchovy sauce in a blender and puree until smooth. Pour the puree in a small mixing bowl. Add Korean chili flakes, sugar, and Koran plum extract for tea, if using. Mix well.

Place drained cabbages in a large shallow mixing bowl. Add the red chilies if using, and the kimchi filling. Toss all together to coat evenly. Sprinkle toasted sesame seeds and toss well. Adjust seasoning as you wish.

This kimchi will stay fresh in the fridge for 10 days. Not ideal for a long term fermentation.

KIMCHI TUNA RICE PATTIES AND BALLS

Ingredients

1 cup very fermented sour kimchi chopped

1 (5oz, 145g) canned tuna, drained well

3 tablespoon kimci juice

2 green onion, chopped

1 teaspoon sesame oil

toasted white and black sesame seeds

4 cups cooked short grain white rice

1-2 sheets plain roasted seaweeds

(seasoned and roasted seaweeds for rice balls)

Directions

Sauté kimchi in kimchi juice over medium heat for 2 minutes. Add tuna and stir to continue sautéing until kimchi is somewhat soft and the mixture seems a little dry.

Add green onion and heat through. Add sesame oil and stir. Set aside to cool a little.

Season rice with a couple of pinches of salt.

In a rice patty presser, fill rice to halfway up. place a tablespoonful of kimchi tuna filling over the rice leaving edges and corners untouched. Fill more rice on top to cover to the rim of the presser. Cover the lid and press down. Uncover and release the patty by pushing the bottom of the press.

Cut a sheet of plain roasted seaweed into 8 strips. Wrap the bottom of the rice patties with the seaweed strips.

Dip the top of rice patties in roasted sesame seeds to coat.

To make rice balls, mix kimchi tuna filling, 1 tablespoon sesame seeds with rice. Roll the mixture to make small balls.

Crush seasoned roasted seaweeds in plastic bags until they get crushed into small pieces. Roll the rice balls to coat with seaweeds.

RADISH KIMCHI

Ingredients

1-1/2 lb (700g) Korean radish

1-1/2cup (400ml) sprite

1/3 cup Korean coarse sea salt

2 tablespoon cooked and mashed potato

3 garlic cloves

1/2" piece ginger

1 small onion

1/2 cup Korean chili flakes

2 tablespoon salted shrimp

1 tablespoon anchovy sauce

1 tablespoon sugar

salt to taste, optional

For the anchovy stock;

5-6 dried large anchovies

1 piece (size or your palm) dried sea kelp

1 cup water

Directions

 Peel the radish and slice them from the side to center as you pivot the radish to create one side thicker than the other, about 1/2" thick on the top.

In a large shallow bowl dissolve salt in Sprite. Add the radish slices and soak for 1 hour. Toss radishes a couple of times during to get evenly salted.

To make a stock, combine anchovies and sea kelp with about 1 cup water in a pot and bring to boil, simmer for 10 minutes. Remove from heat and let it rest until ready to use.

In a blender combine garlic, ginger, onion, mashed potato, and pour 1/2 cup of anchovy stock. Puree until smooth.

When the radishes are done with soaking rinse them a couple of times. Drain well.

In a small mixing bowl, combine chili flakes, salted shrimp, anchovy sauce, sugar, and the onion garlic puree. Mix well to form thin batter.

In a large shallow mixing bowl, combine radishes and the chili filling. Toss well to coat. You just made a wonderful radish kimchi!

Transfer the radish kimchi into an airtight container. Pour 1/2 cup of water to the mixing bowl you used to rinse out the entire remaining chili filling. Pour the chili juice over the radish Kimchi.

Cover and let it sit in the room temperature for 1-2 days. You will see more water is coming out of radishes. Toss well to even out the juice. Store the kimchi in the fridge for 1 week and your radish kimchi is ready to serve!

PERILLA LEAF KIMCHI,

Ingredients

about 50 Perilla leaves

1/2 onion, thinly sliced

1/2 carrot, sliced into thin matchsticks

2 red chilies

3/4 cup anchovy stock*

3 tablespoon Korean chili flakes

2 tablespoon Korean fish sauce

1 tablespoon Korean soy sauce for soup

1 tablespoon sugar Coupons

1 tablespoon Korean corn syrup, optional

1 tablespoon garlic, finely minced

2 teaspoon toasted sesame seeds

* anchovy stock: simmer 4-5 dried large anchovies and a piece of dried sea kelp in 1 1/2 cup of water for 10 minutes.

Directions

Clean Perilla leaves in water thoroughly. Drain well to remove excess water. (Use a salad spinner if you own)

In a small mixing bowl combine chopped fresh chilies, Korean chili flakes, fish sauce, soy sauce for soup, sugar, corn syrup if using, garlic, and sesame seeds. Add 1/2 cup of anchovy stock to the mixture and stir well. The seasoning paste will be runny.

Place a Perilla leaf on the shallow plate (I use a glass pie dish) spread 1 teaspoonful of seasoning paste around on top of leaf. Sprinkle a few slices of onion and carrots on top. Place another 2-3 leaves on top and repeat the layer. You don't need to spread the seasoning on every leaf. Stack them in a air tight container.

Pour 1/4 cup of remaining anchovy stock to the seasoning paste, swirl around, and pour over the leaves. Press down gently with a spoon.

Let the Kimchi sit on the room temperature for 1 day and store in the fridge afterwards. Serve with rice as a side dish.

KIMCHI MARINADE

Ingredients

1/2 cup chopped Korean pear

1/2 cup gochugaru (Korean red chili flakes), coarsely ground

1/4 cup fish sauce

2 garlic cloves, minced

2 tablespoons sugar

2 teaspoons minced ginger

CURE MIX

3 tablespoons sugar

3 tablespoons Kosher salt

Preparation

First, make the marinade: Add the pear, gochugaru, fish sauce, garlic, sugar and ginger to a blender and blend until smooth.

Then, make the cure mix, which draws out extra liq uid and adds additional seasoning: In a small bowl, stir together the sugar and salt.

KIMCHI GRILLED CORN ON THE COB

YIELD: 4-6 servings

PREP TIME: 5 minutes

COOK TIME: 10 minutes

Ingredients:

4-6 ears fresh Florida Sweet Corn

1 cup prepared kimchi

¼ cup melted butter

2 tablespoons honey

Salt

Directions:

Preheat the grill to high heat. Remove the cornhusks and corn silk, and lay the fresh Florida Sweet Corn on a rimmed baking dish.

Place the kimchi in a food processor or high-powered blender. Pulse until the kimchi is finely chopped. Then add the melted butter, honey and salt to taste. Puree until smooth.

Brush the kimchi mixture onto the ears of corn, coating completely. Then place the corn on the grill. Grill for 8-10 minutes, turning the corn every 2 minutes until all sides are slightly charred. Remove and serve warm.

Notes: If you don't own a grill you can achieve similar results by cooking the corn in a large cast iron skillet over high heat. Make sure the skillet is piping hot before adding the corn.

KIMCHI GRILLED CHEESE

Ingredients

4 slices of your favorite bread

2 tbsp butter, softened (or enough to thinly butter one side of each slice)

4 slices American cheese

3/4 to 1 cup kimchi, drained, patted dry, and chopped

Instructions

Butter one side of each slice of bread, taking care to spread the butter to the very edges.

Note: You can also melt the butter directly into the skillet and then fry the bread in it, which is handy especially if you're like me and tend to forget to soften the butter beforehand.

Heat a skillet over medium-low heat, then place two slices of bread butter-side down. (If you'd like to go the melted-butter route, add about 1 tbsp of the butter, swirl it until melted, then add the bread.)

Next, add one slice of cheese to each slice of bread.

Layer kimchi over the cheese, then add a second slice to each.

Let the bread fry on the skillet until golden-brown and the cheese begins to melt on top. Depending on your skillet, you may want to lower the heat to low to prevent burning

Add the uncooked slices of bread, buttered-side up, to complete the sandwiches, then gently flip the sandwiches to their uncooked sides. (If they're not buttered, add the uncooked slices, remove from the pan, add the remaining 1 tbsp of butter to the pan to melt, and then add the sandwiches back to the pan, uncooked side down.)

Continue to let cook in the pan for a minute or so longer, until the uncooked sides are golden-brown. Remove and let cool, then slice and serve!

KIMCHI SCRAMBLE

INGREDIENTS

Extra virgin olive oil

Eggs, lightly beaten

Kale leaves, thick stems removed, torn into thumb-sized pieces

Kimchi (use your favorite flavor — i love the traditional cabbage, green onion, and daikon radish)

Mung bean or alfalfa sprouts (optional)

Chia or hemp seeds (optional)

INSTRUCTIONS:

Heat oil in a wok or a saute pan over medium until shimmering. Swirl the oil in the pan to coat the bottom and up a bit of the sides. Add the eggs and reduce heat to medium-low. Stir constantly as the eggs cook. When nearly cooked through, add the kale. Keep the eggs and kale moving around the pan.

When the kale turns a bright green and is slightly wilted, add the kimchi and sprouts (if using) and the cooked quinoa. Give everything a good stir and heat for an additional minute or two.

Spoon onto plates, and sprinkle with chia seeds, if desired.

SPICY KIMCHI FRITTATA

INGREDIENTS

2 tablespoons olive oil

5 eggs

Half cup low fat milk

2 teaspoons pepper

2 tablespoons chopped kimchi

Half cup sliced shitaki mushrooms

2 tablespoons diced scallions

DIRECTION

Preheat oven to 350 Add 1 tablespoon of olive oil to a pan.

Saute Whisk together eggs, milk and pepper in a bowl Pour egg batter into mini ovenproof dishes (cast iron or stoneware).

Place diced kimchi, mushrooms and scallions on top of frittata.

Bake in oven until eggs are just set. 15 minutes.

Serve warm.

CHAPTER EIGHT

CHUTNEY SALSAS AND RELISHES RECIPES

CARAMELISED ONION CHUTNEY

Ingredients

Serves: 20

7 medium red onions

2 medium shallots

1 medium white onion

1 sweet pepper (red or orange; grilled until black, peeled, seeded and diced)

1 red chili, seeded and diced

270ml balsamic vinegar

50ml red wine vinegar

220g dark brown sugar

7cm stick cinnamon

2 fresh bay leaves

1 large sprig of rosemary, leaves picked and chopped

Olive oil

Method

Prep:25min › Cook:1hr30min › Extra time:5min › Ready in:2hr

Peel and chop the onions and shallots into chutney size pieces, add olive oil to a pan add the onions, bay leaves, cinnamon and rosemary.

Cook for about 20mins on a low heat until the onions are golden, soft and sticky, add the chili and pepper cook for a further couple of mins.

Add the vinegar and sugar; simmer on a low heat until thick and chutney like.

Spoon into sterilized jars.Can be left for 4-6 weeks to develop flavour.

CORIANDER CHUTNEY

Ingredients

Serves: 4

1 bunch fresh coriander

1 clove garlic

1 tablespoon minced fresh root ginger

1 minced green chili

1 tablespoon peanuts

Salt to taste

2 tablespoons lemon juice

Method

Prep:10min › Ready in:10min

Blend all ingredients in a food processor until smooth. Add a few drops of water if the mixture is too dry.

MEXICAN SALSA RECIPE

MAKES:

14 servings

TOTAL TIME:

Prep: 40 min.

INGREDIENTS

3 jalapeno peppers

1 medium onion, quartered

1 garlic clove, halved

2 cans (one 28 ounces, one 14-1/2 ounces) whole tomatoes, drained

4 fresh cilantro sprigs

1/2 teaspoon salt

DIRECTIONS

Heat a small ungreased cast-iron skillet over high heat. With a small sharp knife, pierce jalapenos; add to hot skillet. Cook for 15-20 minutes or until peppers are blistered and blackened, turning occasionally.

Immediately place jalapenos in a small bowl; cover and let stand for 20 minutes. Peel off and discard charred skins. Remove stems and seeds.

Place onion and garlic in a food processor; cover and pulse four times. Add the tomatoes, cilantro, salt and jalapenos.

Cover and process until desired consistency. Chill until serving. Serve with chips. Yield: 3-1/2 cups.

AVOCADO SALSA RECIPE

MAKES:

28 servings

TOTAL TIME:

Prep: 20 min. + chilling

INGREDIENTS

1-2/3 cups (about 8-1/4 ounces) frozen corn, thawed

2 cans (2-1/4 ounces each) sliced ripe olives, drained

1 medium sweet red pepper, chopped

1 small onion, chopped

5 garlic cloves, minced

1/3 cup olive oil

1/4 cup lemon juice

3 tablespoons cider vinegar

1 teaspoon dried oregano

1/2 teaspoon salt

1/2 teaspoon pepper

4 medium ripe avocados, peeled

Tortilla chips

DIRECTIONS

Combine corn, olives, red pepper and onion. In another bowl, mix the next seven ingredients. Pour over corn mixture; toss to coat. Refrigerate, covered, overnight.

Just before serving, chop avocados; stir into salsa. Serve with tortilla chips. Yield: about 7 cups.

GARDEN SALSA RECIPE

MAKES:

40 servings

TOTAL TIME:

Prep/Total Time: 15 min.

INGREDIENTS

6 medium tomatoes, finely chopped

3/4 cup finely chopped green pepper

1/2 cup finely chopped onion

1/2 cup thinly sliced green onions

6 garlic cloves, minced

2 teaspoons cider vinegar

2 teaspoons lemon juice

2 teaspoons olive oil

1 to 2 teaspoons minced jalapeno pepper

1 to 2 teaspoons ground cumin

1/2 teaspoon salt

1/4 to 1/2 teaspoon cayenne pepper

Tortilla chips

DIRECTIONS

In a large bowl, combine the tomatoes, green pepper, onions, garlic, vinegar, lemon juice, oil, jalapeno and seasonings. Cover and refrigerate until serving. Serve with chips. Yield: 5 cups.

SPICY CHUNKY SALSA RECIPE

TOTAL TIME: Prep: 1-1/2 hours Process: 15 min. MAKES: 64 servings

Ingredients

6 pounds tomatoes

3 large green peppers, chopped

3 large onions, chopped

2 cups white vinegar

1 large sweet red pepper, chopped

1 can (12 ounces) tomato paste

4 jalapeno peppers, seeded and chopped

2 serrano peppers, seeded and chopped

1/2 cup sugar

1/2 cup minced fresh cilantro

1/2 cup bottled lemon juice

3 garlic cloves, minced

4 teaspoons ground cumin

1 tablespoon salt

2 teaspoons dried oregano

1 teaspoon hot pepper sauce

Directions

In a Dutch oven, bring 2 quarts water to a boil. Using a slotted spoon, place tomatoes, a few at a time, in boiling water for 30-60 seconds. Remove each tomato and immediately plunge into ice water. Drain and pat dry. Peel and finely chop tomatoes to measure 9 cups; place in a stockpot.

Stir in remaining ingredients. Add water to cover; bring to a boil. Reduce heat; simmer, uncovered, until slightly thickened, about 30 minutes.

Ladle hot mixture into hot 1-pint jars, leaving 1/2-in. headspace. Remove air bubbles and adjust headspace, if necessary, by adding hot mixture. Wipe rims. Center lids on jars; screw on bands until fingertip tight.

Place jars into canner with simmering water, ensuring that they are completely covered with water. Bring to a boil; process for 15 minutes. Remove jars and cool. Yield: 8 pints.

CREAMY BLACK BEAN SALSA RECIPE

MAKES:

16 servings

TOTAL TIME:

Prep/Total Time: 20 min.

INGREDIENTS

1 can (15 ounces) black beans, rinsed and drained

1-1/2 cups frozen corn, thawed

1 cup finely chopped sweet red pepper

3/4 cup finely chopped green pepper

1/2 cup finely chopped red onion

1 tablespoon minced fresh parsley

1/2 cup sour cream

1/4 cup mayonnaise

2 tablespoons red wine vinegar

1 teaspoon ground cumin

1 teaspoon chili powder

1/2 teaspoon salt

1/4 teaspoon garlic powder

1/8 teaspoon pepper

Tortilla chips

DIRECTIONS

In a large bowl, combine the beans, corn, peppers, onion and parsley. Combine the sour cream, mayonnaise, vinegar and seasonings; pour over corn mixture and toss gently to coat. Serve with tortilla chips. Refrigerate leftovers. Yield: 4 cups.

MANGO PINEAPPLE SALSA RECIPE

TOTAL TIME: Prep: 10 min. + chilling MAKES: 10 servings

Ingredients

1 cup chopped peeled mango

1 cup pineapple tidbits

1/2 cup diced sweet red pepper

1 plum tomato, seeded and chopped

3 tablespoons minced fresh cilantro

2 green onions, sliced

2 tablespoons lime juice

1 tablespoon lemon juice

1 jalapeno pepper, finely chopped

Tortilla chips

Directions

In a large bowl, combine the first nine ingredients. Cover and refrigerate for 1 hour or until chilled. Serve with tortilla chips. Yield: 2-2/3 cups.

FRUIT SALSA WITH CINNAMON CHIPS RECIPE

TOTAL TIME: Prep/Total Time: 30 min. MAKES: 20 servings

Ingredients

1 cup finely chopped fresh strawberries

1 medium navel orange, peeled and finely chopped

3 medium kiwifruit, peeled and finely chopped

1 can (8 ounces) unsweetened crushed pineapple, drained

1 tablespoon lemon juice

1-1/2 teaspoons sugar

CINNAMON CHIPS:

10 flour tortillas (8 inches)

1/4 cup butter, melted

1/3 cup sugar

1 teaspoon ground cinnamon

Directions

In a small bowl, combine the first six ingredients. Cover and refrigerate until serving.

For chips, brush tortillas with butter; cut each into eight wedges. Combine sugar and cinnamon; sprinkle over tortillas. Place on ungreased baking sheets.

Bake at 350° for 5-10 minutes or just until crisp. Serve with fruit salsa. Yield: 2-1/2 cups salsa (80 chips).

MILD TOMATO SALSA RECIPE

TOTAL TIME: Prep: 40 min. + simmering Process: 20 min.
MAKES: 160 servings

Ingredients

10-1/2 pounds tomatoes (about 35 medium), peeled and
q uartered

4 medium green peppers, chopped

3 large onions, chopped

2 cans (12 ounces each) tomato paste

1-3/4 cups white vinegar

1/2 cup sugar

1 medium sweet red pepper, chopped

1 celery rib, chopped

15 garlic cloves, minced

4 to 5 jalapeno peppers, seeded and chopped

1/4 cup canning salt

1/4 to 1/2 teaspoon hot pepper sauce

Directions

In a large stockpot, cook tomatoes, uncovered, over medium
heat 20 minutes. Drain, reserving 2 cups liquid. Return
tomatoes to the pot.

Stir in green peppers, onions, tomato paste, vinegar, sugar,
red pepper, celery, garlic, jalapenos, canning salt, hot pepper

sauce and reserved tomato liq uid. Bring to a boil. Reduce heat; simmer, uncovered, 1 hour, stirring freq uently.

Ladle hot mixture into 10 hot 1-pint jars, leaving 1/2-in. headspace. Remove air bubbles and adjust headspace, if necessary, by adding hot mixture. Wipe rims. Center lids on jars; screw on bands until fingertip tight.

Place jars into canner with simmering water, ensuring that they are completely covered with water. Bring to a boil; process for 20 minutes. Remove jars and cool. Yield: 10 pints.

CORN RELISH

Ingredients

2 cups whole kernel corn

1/4 cup chopped green bell peppers

1/2 onion, thinly sliced 6 tablespoons sweet pickle relish

1/4 teaspoon celery seed

1/2 teaspoon salt

1/4 teaspoon dry mustard

2 tablespoons distilled white vinegar

2 tablespoons white corn syrup

Directions

In a medium saucepan, mix together the corn, green bell peppers, onion, sweet pickle relish, celery seed, salt, dry mustard, vinegar and corn syrup. Bring to a boil, reduce heat and simmer 5 minutes.

HOMEMADE SWEET ZUCCHINI RELISH

Ingredients

10 small zucchini,

Ends trimmed 1 red bell pepper,

stemmed and seeded 4 onions, peeled

3 tablespoons salt

4 cups white sugar

2 1/4 cups vinegar

1 teaspoon celery seed

1 teaspoon ground turmeric

1/4 cup cornstarch

12 half pint canning jars with lids and rings .

Directions

Run zucchini, red bell pepper, and onions through a meat grinder. Transfer ground zucchini mixture to a large bowl; sprinkle with salt. Refrigerate zucchini mixture, overnight or at least 10 hours.

Pour zucchini mixture into a large pot; add sugar, vinegar, celery seed, and turmeric. Bring to a boil, stirring constantly, for 15 to 20 minutes. Stir cornstarch into mixture; continue boiling until thickened, about 5 more minutes.

Sterilize the jars and lids in boiling water for at least 5 minutes. Pack relish into the hot, sterilized jars, filling the jars to within 1/4 inch of the top. Run a knife or a thin spatula around the insides of the jars after they have been filled to remove any air bubbles. Wipe the rims of the jars with a moist paper towel to remove any food residue. Top with lids, and screw on rings.

Place a rack in the bottom of a large stockpot and fill halfway with water. Bring to a boil and lower jars into the boiling water using a holder. Leave a 2-inch space between the jars. Pour in more boiling water if necessary to bring the water level to at least 1 inch above the tops of the jars. Bring the water to a rolling boil, cover the pot, and process for 10 minutes.

Remove the jars from the stockpot and place onto a cloth-covered or wood surface, several inches apart, until cool. Once cool, press the top of each lid with a finger, ensuring that the seal is tight (lid does not move up or down at all). Store in a cool, dark area.

FRESH CHERRY TOMATO RELISH

Ingredients

1/2 cup cherry tomatoes, quartered

1 splash olive oil

1 splash red wine vinegar

1 clove garlic, crushed kosher salt.

Ground black pepper to taste

Directions

Stir tomatoes, olive oil, red wine vinegar, garlic, salt, and pepper together in a bowl. Cover the bowl with plastic wrap and refrigerate until flavors blend and juice accumulates, about 30 minutes.

Strain accumulated juices into a small skillet and transfer tomatoes back to the bowl. Cook juices over medium heat until liquid reduces and sauce has a syrup-like consistency, 2 to 3 minutes. Pour sauce back over tomatoes into bowl and stir.

COCONUT CHUTNEY RECIPE

Cooking Time: 10 mins

Ingredients

Grated coconut (1 cup)

Green chilies (2 to 3 pieces)

Curd (1/2 cup)

Salt (as per taste)

Ginger (1 inch pieces)

Garlic (5 to 7 cloves)

Water (as req uired)

Cumin seed (2 teaspoon)

Preparation

Chop chilies and ginger

Peel garlic and put all ingredients in mixer jar except water.

Grind in the mixer grinder.

Add water if you want, q uantity of water is dependent upon what consistency you want.

TAMARIND CHUTNEY RECIPE

Cooking Time: 10 mins

Ingredients

Tamarind seedless(5 teaspoon)

Garlic (6 to 7 cloves)

Red chili powder(2 teaspoon)

Coriander powder(2 teaspoon)

Jaggery (7 teaspoon)

Salt (2 teaspoon)

Preparation

Sock Tamarind in 1 cup of water for 10 to 15 minutes.

Chop jaggery in small pieces.

In mixer jar add Tamarind, jaggery , garlic cloves, chili powder, salt,coriander powder, cumin powder and make fine paste. If req uired add more water.

ONION CHUTNEY RECIPE

Cooking Time: 5 mins

Ingredients

Onion (2 to 3 pieces)

Cumin seeds(2 teaspoon)

Red chili powder (2 to 3 teaspoon)

Salt (as per taste)

Oil (2 teaspoon)

Coriander powder (2 teaspoon)

Water (1/2 cup)

Preparation

Peel and cut onion.

In mixer jar add onion, cumin seeds, red chili powder, salt, coriander powder and make fine paste.

Add water as per req uired.

Heat oil in a pan.

Add prepared chutney.

Sauté for a minute.

CORIANDER CHUTNEY RECIPE

Cooking Time: 8 mins

Ingredients

Coriander leaves (1 cup)

Grated coconut (1 cup)

Green chilies (2 to 3 pieces)

Salt (as per taste)

Lemon juice (2 teaspoon)

Ginger (1 inch pieces)

Garlic (5 to 7 cloves)

Water (as required)

Cumin seed (2 teaspoon)

Preparation

Chop coriander leaves, chilies, ginger.

Peel garlic cloves.

In mixer jar add chopped coriander leaves, chilies, ginger, peeled garlic cloves and grated coconut, salt, cumin seeds.

In mixer grinder make fine paste

Add water to the paste as per required consistency.

At last add lemon and mix well, lemon helps chutney to give different and delicious taste.

Coriander chutney is ready.

TOMATO CHUTNEY RECIPE

Cooking Time: 5mins

Ingredients

Onion (1 to 2 pieces)

Tomato (2 to 3 pieces)

Mustard seeds(1 teaspoon)

Cumin seeds(2 teaspoon)

Red chili powder (2 to 3 teaspoon)

Salt (as per taste)

Oil (2 teaspoon)

Coriander powder (2 teaspoon)

Water (1/2 cup)

Urad dal /split black gram (1 teaspoon)

Curry leaves (5 to 10 leaves)

Preparation

Chop onion and tomato .

Heat oil in the pan and add asafetida .

Add urad dal and sauté till Dal turns pink in color.

Add onion and sauté till it becomes transparent.

Add tomato and sauté for a minute.

Add red chili powder, salt, coriander powder and switch off the flame.

Take this preparation in mixer jar and make a fine paste and add water as per req uired. Add mustard seeds and cumin seeds and sizzle.

Add curry leaves and paste and saute for a minute.

GARLIC CHUTNEY RECIPE

Cooking Time: 6 mins

Ingredients

Garlic (25 to 30 cloves)

Chili powder (5 to 6 teaspoons)

Cumin powder(4 to 5 teaspoon)

Coriander powder (3 teaspoon)

Salt (as per taste)

Oil (3 teaspoon)

Preparation

Peel garlic cloves.

In mixer jar add garlic cloves, chili powder, cumin powder, coriander powder and salt .

Make fine paste in mixer grinder (do not add water).

Heat oil on a medium flame and add paste and switch off flame and mix well.

 Garlic chutney is now ready to serve.

You can preserve this chutney for 10 to 15 days

Pakoda Chutney Recipe

Cooking Time: 12 mins

Ingredients

For Chutney

Garlic (8 to 10 cloves)

Chili powder (2 to 3 teaspoons)

Cumin powder(2 to 3 teaspoon)

Coriander powder (3 teaspoon)

Salt (as per taste)

for Pakoda

Chickpea flour (1 cup)

Salt (as per taste)

Water (1 1\2 cups)

Oil (for frying)

Preparation

We will prepare Pakoda first.

Take chickpea flour,salt and water. Mix them well and form fine batter.

Heat oil in the pan and with the help of spoon or directly by your hand make   Pakoda from batter.

Fry pakoda on a medium flame till pakoda become crispy.

Take all pakoda in mixer jar add garlic, chili powder, cumin seed powder, coriander seed powder and make paste out of it.

 Pakoda chutney is ready to serve.

You can enjoy it with Vada Paav, Roti and other Pakoda dishes.

CHAPTER NINE

AMERICAN HOME MADE DISHES WITH DIFFERENT PICKLED FOODS

GRILLED CHICKEN WITH MANGO-PINEAPPLE SALSA

4 servings (serving size: 1 chicken breast half, 1 tablespoon sauce, and 1/4 cup salsa)

Top grilled chicken breast halves with a sweet-and-spicy tropical salsa of fresh pineapple, mango, jalapeño peppers, and cilantro. Serve over rice for an easy one-dish meal.

Ingredients

Salsa:

2/3 cup diced peeled ripe mango (1 medium)

2/3 cup diced fresh pineapple

2 tablespoons minced red onion

1 tablespoon minced seeded jalapeño pepper

1 1/2 teaspoons chopped fresh cilantro

1 1/2 teaspoons fresh lime juice

1/8 teaspoon salt

1/8 teaspoon freshly ground black pepper

Chicken:

4 (6-ounce) skinless, boneless chicken breast halves

1/4 cup pineapple juice

3 tablespoons chopped fresh cilantro

3 tablespoons low-sodium soy sauce

2 tablespoons honey

1 teaspoon fresh lime juice

Dash of crushed red pepper

Cooking spray

How to Make It

To prepare salsa, combine first 8 ingredients. Cover; refrigerate 30 minutes.

To prepare chicken, place each chicken breast half between 2 sheets of heavy-duty plastic wrap; pound to 1/2-inch thickness using a meat mallet or small heavy skillet. Combine pineapple juice and next 5 ingredients (through red pepper) in a large zip-top plastic bag. Add chicken to bag; seal. Marinate in refrigerator 30 minutes.

Prepare grill.

Remove chicken from bag, reserving marinade. Place chicken on a grill rack coated with cooking spray; grill 3 minutes on each side or until done.

Place reserved marinade in a small saucepan; bring to a boil. Reduce heat, and cook until reduced to 1/4 cup (about 5 minutes). Drizzle over chicken. Serve salsa with chicken.

BACON AND KIMCHI FRIED RICE FRITTATA

Serves 6

1/2 pound thick bacon, cut into 1-inch pieces

1 1/2 cus shiitake mushrooms, coarsely chopped

2 cloves garlic, minced

1/2-inch knob ginger, minced (about 1/2 tablespoon)

1/2 teaspoon kosher salt, divided

1 1/2 teaspoons gochujang

1 cup kimchi

1 cup leftover (medium-grain) cooked rice, at least a day old

1 tablespoon kimchi liq uid

1 cup packed pea shoots, plus additional for garnish

7 eggs

2 tablespoons milk

Grapeseed or olive oil

METHOD

Heat a 10-inch oven-safe skillet over medium-high heat, add the bacon, and allow to render and crisp up. Once the bacon is lightly crisp, add the shiitake mushrooms and cook for 3 to 5 minutes, stirring freq uently. Next add in the garlic, ginger, 1/4 teaspoon of the salt, and gochujang; cook until everything is fragrant.

Firmly sq ueeze the kimchi to remove any liq uid and reserve. Coarsely chop kimchi and add to the skillet. Sauté for one minute; the kimchi should still be crunchy. Turn the heat up to high, add the rice, and stir constantly, making sure that each grain of rice separates, 5 to 8 minutes. Turn off the heat and add in the kimchi liq uid and pea shoots. Gently stir until pea shoots begin to wilt. Transfer to a separate bowl and allow cooling for 10 minutes.

In a large mixing bowl, combine 1/4 teaspoon of the salt, eggs, and the milk. Beat until combined. Stir in the cooled bacon and vegetable mixture.

Heat the oven to 400°F. In the same pan that the rice was cooked in, heat a thin layer of oil over medium-high heat until a drop of egg sizzles and sets within seconds of being added to the pan. Mix the frittata mixture and pour into the pan. Shake the pan gently to get everything to settle in. Cook for a minute undisturbed. Tilt the pan slightly and use a rubber spatula to gently lift up the sides of the frittata, allowing the uncooked eggs to run underneath. After 2 to 3 minutes, a few layers of the eggs will have cooked and the edges will have begun to set; turn the stove off.

Place the pan into the middle of the oven. Bake 10 to 12 more minutes, or until the eggs are just set, rotating the pan halfway through.

Heat the broiler. Broil the frittata for 1 to 3 minutes. Make sure that the eggs aren't too close to the broiler or else they will burn. The frittata should brown slightly and puff up. Remove from the oven, and let stand 5 minutes. Cut and serve directly from the pan or slide onto a large serving plate. Top with additional fresh pea shoots.

ONION CHUTNEY GRILLED CHEESE SANDWICH

Ingredients

2 slices bread

1 tablespoon butter (room temperature)

2 slices cheese (cheddar, gruyere, etc.)

2 tablespoons onion chutney

Directions

Assemble the sandwich and grill until the bread is golden brown and the cheese has melted.

STEAMED RICE WITH PICKLED JAPANESE PLUMS

INGREDIENTS

1 1/2 cups medium-grain Japanese rice

2 pitted umeboshi (Japanese pickled plums), cut into 1/4-inch dice

Get Ingredients

HOW TO MAKE THIS RECIPE

In a bowl, cover the rice with water. Swish the rice vigorously, and then drain off the milky water. Repeat 3 more times, until the water runs nearly clear, then let the rice stand in a fine sieve for 30 minutes.

Transfer the rice to a small saucepan and add 1 1/2 cups plus 2 tablespoons of water. Cover and bring to a boil over high heat. Reduce the heat to low and cook until the water is just absorbed, about 15 minutes. Keeping the pan covered, remove the rice from the heat and let stand for 10 minutes.

Using a moistened rice paddle or wooden spoon, gently fold the plums into the rice. Serve right away.

SKILLET STROGANOFF AND RICE WITH PICKLED ONION

Cook this recipe in 6 simple steps

1. Prep ingredients

Halve, peel, and thinly slice onion. Trim stems from mushrooms and thinly slice caps. Peel and finely chop garlic. Pick parsley leaves from stems and finely chop stems.

2. Pickle onions

Combine vinegar, half of the onion, 1 teaspoon sugar, and ½ teaspoon salt in a small bowl and stir to combine.

3. Brown beef

Heat 1 tablespoon oil in a large skillet over medium-high. Add ground beef and season with pepper and ½ teaspoon salt. Cook, breaking up with a wooden spoon, until deeply browned in spots and cooked through, about 5 minutes. Using a slotted spoon, transfer beef to a bowl.Spoon off all but 1 tablespoon of fat from the skillet.

4. Cook onion and mushrooms

Add 1 tablespoon oil to the skillet then add garlic, mushrooms, and remaining sliced onion. Season with ½ teaspoon salt and cook, stirring often, until golden and softened, 5–7 minutes.

5. Finish skillet

Add rice and paprika to skillet and cook, stirring to combine, about 1 minute. Add Dijon mustard, parsley stems, beef, and

1¼ cups water. Bring to a boil, reduce heat to a simmer, and cover tightly with a lid or foil. Cook until liquid has evaporated and rice is tender, 15–20 minutes.

6. Finish

Toss parsley leaves with pickled onions. Serve stroganoff topped with pickled onions, parsley, and a dollop of sour cream. Serve remaining sour cream on the side. Enjoy!

GREEN ASPARAGUS WITH TOMATO SALSA

INGREDIENTS

800g Baby Coliban (Chat) potatoes, halved (see note)

60ml (1/4 cup) water

4 (about 150g each) firm white fish cutlets or fillets (such as blue-eye trevalla or barramundi)

Olive oil spray

1 bunch asparagus, woody ends trimmed, cut into 3cm lengths

1 x 150g pkt Gourmet Lettuce

100g snow peas, trimmed, thinly shredded

1 Lebanese cucumber, coarsely chopped

Lime wedges, to serve

SALSA

2 large ripe tomatoes, quartered, deseeded, finely chopped

6 pitted kalamata olives, finely chopped

2 tablespoons finely shredded fresh basil

1 teaspoon olive oil

1 tablespoon fresh lime juice

METHOD

Step 1

Place the potato in a shallow microwave-safe dish. Add the water. Cover and cook on High/800Watts/100% for 10 minutes or until tender.

Step 2

Meanwhile, preheat a chargrill or barbecue flat plate on medium. Spray both sides of the fish with olive oil spray. Season with pepper. Cook on grill for 3-4 minutes each side or until golden and the fish flakes when tested with a fork.

Step 3

While the fish is cooking, cook the asparagus in a saucepan of boiling water for 1 minute or until bright green and tender crisp. Refresh under cold running water. Drain. Place the asparagus, lettuce, snow peas and cucumber in a bowl and toss to combine.

Step 4

To make the salsa, combine the tomato, olive, basil, oil and lime juice in a small bowl. Season with pepper.

Step 5

Divide the potato and fish among serving plates. Top with the salsa. Serve with lime wedges and the salad.

GINGER-GLAZED PORK BELLY WITH PICKLED PEAR AND SPINACH SALAD

Preparation: 15 minutes (plus 30 minutes pickling time)

Cooking: 2 hours 30 minutes

FOR THE PICKLED PEARS

INGREDIENTS

125ml (1/2 cup) white wine vinegar

1/3 cup sugar

1 cinnamon q uill, broken in half

4 star anise

6 cloves

2 firm pears

METHOD

1. Put the vinegar, sugar, cinnamon, star anise and cloves in a saucepan with 60ml water. Bring to the boil, stirring until the sugar has dissolved. Set aside to cool.

2. Core the pears and slice into thin wedges then pour the cooled pickling mixture over them. Stand for 30 minutes.

FOR THE PORK & SALAD

INGREDIENTS

2kg boneless pork belly, skin scored

2 tablespoons salt

7cm ginger, peeled, grated

1 tablespoon honey

250ml apple juice

1 tablespoon olive oil

400g spinach, shredded, stems discarded

100g hazelnuts, roasted, coarsely chopped

Extra virgin olive oil to serve

METHOD

1. Rub the skin of the pork well with the salt. Place a couple of sheets of paper towel over it to absorb the moisture and leave for 30 minutes to come to room temperature. Preheat the oven to 200°C.

2. In a bowl, combine the ginger, honey and 1 tablespoon of the apple juice. Turn the pork belly flesh side up (use the paper towel to help hold the salt on). Smear the flesh with the ginger mix then put the pork belly on a rack in a roasting dish, skin-side up, and remove the paper towel. Drizzle with the olive oil.

3. Roast for 30 minutes then pour the remaining apple juice and 250ml water into the base of the roasting dish, reduce the oven temperature to 160°C and roast for a further 2 hours.

4. Remove from the oven, take the pork off the rack and sit it in the thickened apple juice mixture in the roasting dish for 20 minutes before carving.

5. For the salad, drain the pears (reserve a little of the syrup) then combine with the spinach and hazelnuts. Drizzle with extra virgin olive oil and toss to combine then drizzle with a little reserved syrup to taste.

SPICY FISH WITH TOMATO SALSA

INGREDIENTS

5 green onions, sliced

4 shallots, chopped

3 beefsteak tomatoes, chopped

2 cloves garlic, minced

1 cup pitted green olives, chopped

1 red bell pepper, chopped

¼ cup capers

1 lime, zest and juice

6 pieces basa or cod fillets

⅓ cup canned chipotles, chopped

½ cup cilantro, chopped

Salt and pepper

2 Tbsp butter, divided

2 Tbsp olive oil

Small flour tortillas (optional)

DIRECTIONS

1. In a large bowl, combine green onions, shallots, tomatoes, garlic, olives, red pepper, and capers. Add zest and squeeze lime juice over mixture; set aside.

2. Rub outside of fish with chipotle; sprinkle with cilantro and season with salt and pepper.

3. Heat butter and oil in a large skillet, fry fish in batches and cook until done, about 6-8 minutes. Place fish on tray and top with salsa mixture.

4. Serve with warm tortillas, if using.

CHICKEN THIGHS WITH SWEET ONION BALSAMIC RELISH

Ingredients

2 teaspoons olive oil

1 lb vidalia onions (3/8 inch sq uare) or 1 lb some other sweet onion, cut into large dice (3/8 inch sq uare)

1/2 teaspoon ground black pepper, divided

4 (6 ounce) skinless chicken thighs

1/4 teaspoon dried oregano

1/2 teaspoon dried thyme

5 teaspoons balsamic vinegar, divided

salt

1 tablespoon chopped parsley (optional)

Directions

Heat the oil in a large nonstick skillet over medium heat.

Saute onions with 1/4 teaspoon of pepper for about 5 minutes, the onions should be soft and golden.

Add 1/4 teaspoon pepper, chicken, oregano, and thyme to pan, and sprinkle with 4 teaspoons balsamic vinegar.

Cover, reduce heat, and simmer 25 minutes or until chicken is done.

Uncover, increase heat, and cook 2 minutes or until liquid almost evaporates.

Stir in 1 teaspoon vinegar, and sprinkle with parsley.

TURKEY STEAM BUNS WITH CUCUMBER-RADISH KIMCHI

Ingredients:

10 oz Ground Turkey

6 Chinese Steam Buns

6 Oz Radishes

3 Cloves Garlic

3 Scallions

1 English Cucumber

2 Tbsp Rice Wine Vinegar

2 Tbsp Sugar

2 Tbsp Ground Bean Sauce

1 1-inch Piece Ginger

1 1/4 Tbsp Gochugaru (Korean Chile Flakes)

1/4 c water

Oil

Salt & Pepper

Instructions (Starting tips and Kimchi):

Heat large pot of water to a boil, maintain boil so water is ready to steam the buns

Slice cucumber and radishes into thin discs, mix into large bowl

Mince garlic and ginger. Add half of the ginger and half of the garlic to the cucumber & radish mix

Thinly slice scallions on an angle. Discard root ends. Separate white ends from green tops. Add half of the green tops to the cucumber & radish mix

Add half of the sugar, half of the gochugaru, the rice wine vinegar, and a drizzle of olive oil to the cucumber & radish mix

Toss mix to thoroughly combine mixture. Salt and pepper to taste. Set aside to marinate, stirring occasionally.

Instructions (Filling):

Heat 2 tsp of oil over medium heat

Cook turkey, breaking apart, until browned

Remove turkey from pan, leaving the fond (browned bits — we learned something!)

Add white bottoms of scallions, remaining garlic and ginger. Stir frequently until softened and fragrant (about a minute)

Add ground bean sauce, cooked turkey, remaining sugar, 1/4 cup of water, and as much as the remaining gochugaru as you'd like

We love spice. We used the whole packet. It wasn't anywhere close to unbearable or too hot.

Cook, stirring occasionally, until thickened

Remove from heat

ground turkey

Steam the Buns:

Placing colander in pot, allowing it to sit above the water, place steam buns in colander.

Cover with lid for 3-5 minutes, steaming the buns until they are soft and puffed

You may need to do this in waves, depending on how big your pot/colander is

Carefully transfer buns to a large plate/clean workspace

steaming buns

Compiling Your Buns:

Stuff as full as you can with kimchi and turkey, garnishing with the left-over green tops of the scallions. Eat extra kimchi on the side. This gets a little messy but it's totally worth it.

www.ingramcontent.com/pod-product-compliance
Lightning Source LLC
LaVergne TN
LVHW010244030325
804941LV00010B/850